A Christmas Tapestry

by *John Johnson* & *Will Johnson*

Arthur M. Kelly, Publishing Coordinator
Cover and Layout by Curtis Corzine

FOREWORD

Unlike mass-produced rugs and carpets, a hand woven tapestry is unique. Design, dyes, wool, and touch—all combine to create a new thing. Every family is a unique tapestry. For the Johnson family, that story is still being woven as each of us tries to determine where we can become of largest use in the Kingdom of God. We have had incredible opportunities, and we are all indebted to a sending church which has validated our ministries, making possible our missions tapestry.

Travel has been our joy and passion. We have stored our wealth in family journeys and lifetime memories in far away places. Our call to be global citizens and ministers of the Word has been a wonderful privilege. We have not wearied in telling the Christmas story to those who need to hear.

John and his family have picked up the thread of mission; they are weaving their own family tapestry. First in South Korea, then in Egypt, and now in Lebanon, they have sensed God working in their lives to make a difference among people who need to know that age old story of Christmas.

While they were living in Egypt, John began some creative writing, inspired by living in the cradle of Christianity. He has incorporated son Will's flair for drawing and asked him to do the illustrations. For several years their Christmas cards have featured Will's artistry. Several of those are beautifully incorporated in this book.

On the back cover is a picture of three generations of Johnsons. They are grandfather, son, and grandson—three persons—three threads woven into a tapestry reflecting a design given by God. Inevitably, the Christmas miracle is at its center.

In the years following September 11, 2001, the Christmas tapestry may seem to have some errant strands. Its bright colors may seem subdued and faded. Could the story told in carefully selected threads and divinely pondered design have changed?

No—recent disturbing events have not changed it!
No—the fear of anthrax or bio-terrorism will not alter it!
No—hatred and violence only illustrate the purpose in the Master Weaver's mind:

"Do not be afraid; for see—
I am bringing you good news of great joy for all people:
to you is born this day in the city of David a Savior,
who is the Messiah, the Lord" (Luke 2:10-11 NRSV).

These words will always and forever be the unchanging theme of *A Christmas Tapestry*.

Donald D. Johnson
October, 2001

CONTENTS

ACKNOWLEDGEMENTS

There are a few people that I really must thank. I am indebted to so many.

The first is Dave Petrescue. Dave was my pastor at Maadi Community Church in Cairo, Egypt. Dave was a constant source of encouragement. Several times during the writing of this book I would pop into Dave's office and read him a piece. Almost without exception, Dave responded with great enthusiasm. He even invited me to share a few of these stories with the congregation at various times throughout the Advent season. Thanks for your encouragement, Dave, and "Pastor Zackery Prepares for Advent" is for you.

Cliff Gardner is another person I must thank. Cliff is the director of the Middle East Studies Program with the Christian College Coalition. When Cliff took his first group into Israel he invited me to tag along. Without that exposure to Israel I would not have been able to write many of these stories. Thank you, Cliff, for including me. The story of "A Christmas Miracle in the Old City" is written especially for you.

Mike and Madelyn Edens are a special gift from God to our family. Their insights into the Middle East and their commitment to long-term ministry to the people of God is a constant source of inspiration to me. One of my special memories of this Christmas season is sitting in the Edens' kitchen reading "A Palestinian Christmas Story." They were the first persons to whom I read that story. We shared a wonderful spontaneous moment of worship together in that kitchen. That story is for you.

Freddie Fadel and I teamed up to present "A Celebration of Christmas through Stories and Songs" at Maadi Community Church during Advent. Freddie's gift as worship leader is only equaled by his divinely-inspired ability to paint. Thank you, Freddie, for your friendship and support. "Do You Hear the Symphony?" is for you.

This collection of short stories would never have come out in a readable and understandable form without my wife, Gwen. Her patient proofreading was a time-consuming and tiring venture. "The Empty Manger" is for you. May our family's Christmas traditions always have Christ at the center.

One more word of thanks. Jonni and Will, my children, were not always thrilled about these stories. They simply are not told in the way that ten-year olds and seven-year olds normally hear the stories of Christmas. Their loving teasing and warm hugs will always be cherished. Since we have seen together the sights described in "The Garbage Collectors' Gifts," that story is for you.

I must add that the pencil drawing on the front of this collection of stories was drawn by Will.
Way to go, Will!

INTRODUCTION

The majority of the carpet schools in Egypt are located along the road that leads to the Step Pyramids just outside Cairo. These are really businesses that sell woolen and silk handmade carpets to foreign tourists. They are called "schools" because children are taught how to weave there and, as such, are the primary work force. The children work at the looms, their dexterous fingers tying knots at a remarkable speed. The children learn a trade and at the same time earn a bit of money for their families. Most of these children tie the knots according to predesigned patterns. What these little carpet-makers come up with are amazing pieces of art, but they are pieces of art, that with time, skill, and patience, can be repeated.

Not far from the carpet schools is the world famous Wisa Wassef Tapestry Workshop. The artists here started as children as well. They, too, were taught the basics of knotting and color selection. But there is a major difference in the end product. All of the tapestries that come off the looms at this workshop are one-of-a-kind masterpieces. The artists, many of whom are now adults, create the everyday scenes of Egypt from scratch. What the artist sees with his eyes and formulates with his mind is woven into a unique design. There are no patterns involved.

The carpet schools and Wisa Wassef Tapestry Workshop both create handmade works of art. The major difference is that the majority of carpets at the carpet schools are made by design. At Wisa Wassef, from an early age, the children are encouraged to create, to weave the world around them.

Christmas is a tapestry. The focal point of this tapestry is Christ. Around the baby in the manger flow many familiar characters: the Holy Family, shepherds, and wise men. This tapestry begins with a set theme: Christ's "in-breaking" into our world; Emmanuel, God with us. So, in a very real way, we could say that Christmas is a tapestry that is by design, God's design created at the "right time" with the "right threads" (Gal 4:4). But by saying that it has been created by design does not mean that it will ever be repeated. It is a once-for-all-time event, a one-of-a-kind tapestry.

In certain areas of Cairo carpets can be found for sale—in carpet school showrooms or in the *suk*, the market. A person can walk into a stall in the *suk*, see and touch hundreds of carpets, and perhaps even enter a protracted discussion with the intent of buying one of these gorgeous works of art. As the potential buyer inquires about the price, the common response is "Pick out the three or four that you like best and later we can discuss the price." The bargaining has begun. When the customer finally hears the price, the wise bargainer might respond, "Surely you must be joking. Remember, I'm not a tourist. I live here in Cairo. A price of ... (he names something only a quarter of the quoted price) is more in line with reality. After all, what is ... (he mentions the three-quarter discount that he is requesting) between you and me?" And so it goes. The actual price will end up somewhere in between the two prices mentioned.

For believers, Christmas isn't just a tapestry to be haggled over. It isn't of value because we acquired it at a good price. It is of value because it is a gift. This tapestry has become ours through faith. What we accept by faith is that ...

- the child in the manger is God's Son, come for us.
- the lowly infant is Emmanuel, God with us.
- the babe of Bethlehem is the very one who grew to be a man, taught about love, and has instructed us as well.
- this Christ never sinned, yet died a criminal's death for our sins.
- this Anointed One from God was resurrected and now sits at the right hand of God to make intercession for us.

The central feature of the Christmas tapestry is Christ. This is God's design. But each one of us has personalized our Christmas tapestry. When the word *Christmas* is mentioned, images other than the biblical accounts and our faith pilgrimage pop into our minds. Special, faithfully-observed traditions, deeply-cherished memories, and wonderful family gatherings set our personal Christmas tapestry apart from all others.

When Christ is at the center of the tapestry, God himself thrills to stand behind us at our loom as we weave and personalize our glorious one-of-a-kind masterpieces. When Christ is absent in our Christmas weavings, the heart of the Master Weaver, God, is broken.

Most of the stories in this collection have a Middle Eastern flavor. This is because they were written in Cairo, Beirut, and Jerusalem. Often we forget that the first Christmas happened in this part of the world. And as much as we try to dress the story up with bathrobes and shepherd's crooks, we still envision Christmas in a western way. It is the intent of this collection to honor Christ, to help you, the reader, see Christmas in a fresh way, and to add a few Middle Eastern touches of color to your Christmas tapestry.

John M. Johnson
Cairo, Egypt
December 1994

A word on how to use these stories—

Most of the stories that appear in *A Christmas Tapestry* were written during a very difficult period in my missionary career. I had been discipling some young men in Egypt for an extended period of time. I was finding great fulfillment in this ministry. Together we had decided to gather a group of young men from all over Egypt during a vacation period for a retreat a few months hence. I was excited. I was going to be helping some very bright, eager young men to better appreciate and understand God's Word. The problem was that I did not involve some of the elder pastors in the planning process. This was clearly a mistake. Not only was the conference cancelled but I received a rather stinging rebuke.

Earlier that fall I had been team teaching a class on the first eleven chapters of Genesis. In preparation for teaching I had written a few stories, more for myself than anyone else, trying to take the ancient creation stories and put them into "modern dress." These stories were often used in the classroom as thought starters and conversation pieces.

When I found myself stymied with regard to the Bible conference for young men, I continued on with my short story writing. It became a personal therapy. I would start each day by reading, studying, reflecting, and writing. As the Christmas season was coming quickly, I began to work on many of the short stories that appear in this book. Upon completing a few I shared them with some of my missionary colleagues and Egyptian friends. The reaction was almost always positive, although I must admit that some of our Egyptian friends were a bit nervous by the fact that I was "tinkering" with God's Holy Word.

What I began to hear from people was that they knew the stories of Christmas so well that the stories no longer had "life" within them. The message had been dulled by repetition. Mary, Joseph, the Angel of the Lord, the shepherds and wise men, Herod and the other Christmas characters had become familiar, so familiar in fact that the power of their faith commitments, the pain and insecurity of their predicament, the good news of their deliverance and vindication had become lost. The wonder of Christmas had been replaced by a rote recitation of the people, places, and events that surrounded the Incarnation. Again and again people told me that the stories had blended together into some sort of children's tale, like *The Golden Book of Christmas*. The story seemed basic, easily understandable, predictable, almost common.

The more that I wrote, the more I would try to weave into the stories the thoughts and setting of Egypt and the Middle East. (After all, was not this the original setting?) Having traveled considerably in Egypt, Palestine, Israel, Jordan, and Lebanon, I tried to consciously reflect the context. In subtle and not so subtle ways, I believe, we have westernized the Christ Event. Like Christian artists from the Middle Ages, we have given the Infant blue eyes and placed him in a European stable.

Conscious of the danger of westernizing Jesus (the reader will have to decide the extent to which I succeeded), I began to wonder what would happen if Jesus were to come into our world of political conflict, social wrangling, greedy manipulation, broken families, and misplaced values. What would happen if Jesus came as a Jew today? What if he were to come to the poorest of the poor in Egypt? What if he were born in a Palestinian refuge camp in war-torn Lebanon?

Not all the stories have been modernized. Many remain in their original setting. I have gone beyond the text to "flesh out" different aspects of the narratives. Other stories have been removed from a Middle Eastern setting. These stories are written to address certain issues like trying to celebrate Christmas without Christ, working to earn our relationship with God, or passing on our faith from generation to generation.

What began as a personal project of healing became a discovery of the meaning of Christmas. As I worked on these stories I was revived. In the midst of my personal and ministry struggles, I found the joy of Christmas. I celebrated the coming of Christ as if I were hearing the stories for the first time. It is my hope that this collection of Christmas stories will be to you a cup of refreshingly cool water on a dry and dusty day.

I believe there are several ways that you might be able to use these stories as:

- a personal advent reading
- conversation starters among small groups
- a personal "refresher course" in the Christmas story
- sermon illustrations
- imagination starters—simply asking the question, "What would it be like if Jesus came today in my context, in my culture?"

However you use them, remember that God's Word and his Christmas story is primary. The stories within *A Christmas Tapestry* are secondary. The Word became flesh is primary and the Word placed in modern dress is secondary. To the extent that these stories aid you in a faithful reading and understanding of the Nativity, to God be the glory.

John M. Johnson
Beirut, Lebanon
November 2001

A Christmas Light

All that existed was tempestuous disorder full of frothing, churning, thundering blackness. Riotous darkness surged and struggled across the planet of God's choosing. And then God breathed forth his Spirit and commanded the light. Transformation ensued. The restless blackness was shattered as light dawned for the first of what would be called "day" in this corner of infinite heavenly spaciousness. It was as if God had taken a sharp knife and, once-and-for-all, separated the oppressive blackness from the life-giving light.

Into this world, now filled with order and light, God placed his children. Amazingly he gave them the freedom to choose light or darkness, radiance or wretchedness, holiness or hell on earth. Amazingly his children again and again opted to live and act under the cover of darkness, choosing a cockroach-like nocturnal existence of demonic disregard. As humanity increased so, too, did the love and hunger for everything in opposition to the God of Light.

Centuries passed. People trudged and labored through life in darkness. For a few brief moments, the light of God broke through. He recreated a people, a community who learned to sing songs about the Lord who was their light and their salvation. God enlightened them as to his character and their purpose: to be a light-giving people to those around them. At times, divinely-inspired voices among the people lifted the sights of many to look forward to that day when all of God's children would finally rise and shine as a result of a decisive coming of the Light. But songs, enlightenment, and prophetic utterance faded as brackish blackness subtly seeped in and swamped and really snuffed out the light within the community.

Still more centuries passed. The people of Nazareth lived in darkened caves. More than that, it was as though all of Palestine had been living through an extended solar eclipse. Light was absent. The place was devoid of hope, joy, freedom, and peace. All that existed in Palestine was tempestuous disorder full of frothing, churning, thundering blackness. Riotous darkness surged and struggled across the land and location of God's choosing. Then God sent forth his Son, the Light of the world. Transformation.

Still more centuries have passed. Jesus Christ, the Christmas Light, has come. The darkness that deforms, destroys, and is devoid of life has been chased away. Its death has been banished, defeated. However, the choice of walking in the Light, being filled with the Light, and shining the Light still remains ours.

Beirut, Lebanon
Merry Christmas 2001

A Tapestry Named "Christmas"

Everyone knows that God is a master artist. He has produced vast symphonies with surging seas, crashing waves, barking sea lions, and singing sea gulls. Such music speaks peace to the soul like nothing else. God has molded delicate pieces of ceramic pottery; infinite detail is his specialty. Then he blows the breath of life into these pieces. A mixture of joy and animation is the result. Often God takes his scissors and intricately cuts pieces of heavenly paper and creates snowflakes. At other times, with agile fingers, God folds colored tissue and brings forth origami-like birds and plants. Sometimes he dons his beret and ventures out to paint a sunset. Pallet in one hand and brush in the other, God paints wide swaths of color across the horizon—brilliant oranges and fiery reds. God is continually unleashing his creative energy. With each blink of his eye, God is producing original masterpieces. Oh yes, God is an artist *extraordinaire*.

On one particular morning God thought to himself, "This is the perfect time to weave a miracle." So God went to his storage room and located his loom. Weaving was one of God's favorite activities. Some might call it God's hobby or past-time, but that really isn't so. Weaving is constantly on God's mind and his fingers literally itch to work the threads.

A smile crossed the face of God. He was finally going to weave the pattern that he had dreamed up before he fashioned the world. With his rich baritone voice God sang as he set about his task.

> O holy night! the stars are brightly shining,
> It is the night of the dear Savior's birth;
> Long lay the world in sin and error pining,
> Till He appeared and the soul felt its worth.
> A thrill of hope the weary world rejoices,
> For yonder breaks a new and glorious morn;
> Fall on your knees, Oh, hear the angel voices!
> O night divine, O night when Christ was born!
> O night, O holy night, O night divine!

19

When God set about the task of weaving, he always followed the same ritual. He would gather all the scraps of his previous weavings first. This way he was careful to fulfill any themes that he had started in years gone by. In a basket by his loom he pulled out a reference to a tiny, insignificant town called Bethlehem. He found a scrap that spoke of a virgin birth. He uncovered the dark threads of the murder of innocents. He shuddered at the thought but included it in the mix that he would weave. Near the bottom of the basket he saw the words, "Cursed is he who is hung on a tree." No, it wasn't time to put this in the weaving, yet he would tint the tapestry just a little with the grays and blacks of that prophecy.

Next God looked out over his world and plucked up threads from the personalities of the day. He found a pure and devoted young woman, a hardworking, honest, and trustworthy carpenter, an elderly couple from a priestly family (the wife was barren), outcast shepherds, expectant kings, and a despicable tyrant who was more concerned about building projects than about his people.

The common and ordinary were not left out. A feed box, white linens, a guest room, money, taxes, a donkey ride, perfume, burial spices, and of course, a child.

Then, in order to blend all these discordant elements together into a whole, God created a special star, sent forth angels, and whispered a few dreams.

Finally God went to his cupboard and reached for woven reed basket labeled "Emotions." He plunged his hand inside and came out with a handful: awe, anger, surprise, hatred, jealousy, fear, bewilderment, wonder, rage, longing, adoration, shock, and fatigue.

Now with these various piles of threads stacked around his loom, God again meditated on the pattern he had concocted so long ago. God mused.

Soon the loom was rocking gently. The shuttle flew back and forth. With each pedal of God's feet and press of his fingers, the weaving began to take shape. Up from the bottom of the frame the tapestry grew, a holy story in the making.

At various times in the process God spoke. Once he said, "*Emmanuel.* Yes, I like that!" Another time as an angel became visible on the carpet, he leaned forward and breathed, "You shall call his name Jesus, for He shall save his people from their sins." When shepherds emerged he spoke again. "Do not be afraid, for I bring you good news of great joy."

From the time God started the work until he finished, he did not leave his stool before the loom. Now finally the last thread was in place. The shuttle became still. The loom quieted. The pedals ceased their stutter-stepping.

God moved back from his masterpiece. He inspected it with great care. It was a worthy piece of art. God entitled the work, "My Kingdom Come."

Today God's tapestry is not so much known by its original name. Often it is simply called "Christmas."

Cairo, Egypt
November 1994

Stories Woven From Matthew's Threads

The Angel of the Lord

Christmas is always such a busy season of the year, what with trying to find the right gift for parents who have everything and need nothing (Why not make a donation in their name to a worthy charity or missions organization?); baking cookies and gingerbread houses (It takes longer with little hands helping but the extra time spent is well worth it); decorating the tree the old-fashioned way with popcorn on a string, colorful paper chains, and home made ornaments; cleaning the house for the guests; making costumes for the Christmas pageant at church; attending musical programs at school; taking a crash course in accounting to see if there's enough money to pay the Visa bill when it comes in February; staying up late the night before Christmas to assemble bikes and insert batteries.... Wow! It's no wonder we are so tired in December.

Just in case we begin to feel sorry for ourselves with our frantic pace during the holiday season, pause for a moment to consider the angel of the Lord. By my count he made four round trips between heaven and earth just in Matthew's Gospel account alone. If we add Luke's Gospel, the number jumps to seven. Think of all those frequent flier miles. Think of the jet lag. I wonder how many time zones there are between heaven and earth? Talk about shuttle diplomacy! My guess is that the angel of the Lord was little concerned with lost luggage or getting caught in the mad holiday rush in airports. From all we can tell, the angel of the Lord traveled lightly. Apparently he didn't even take a carry-on. Maybe it was a little more difficult for the angel band that accompanied the angel of the Lord when he performed his solo in the Shepherd's Field outside of Bethlehem.

No doubt the joy of the message the angel was privileged to announce propelled him through the night sky. Oh, the magnitude of that message! And the expectation of change! When you think about it, the angel was announcing that the earth would now be under new management, the sovereign Master of all was coming to live among humanity. All would behold his glory and they would be changed into his likeness.

Was the angel of the Lord struck by the receptivity of the people that he encountered? With the exception of the old priest Zechariah who was rather set in his ways, each other participant in the Christmas drama was humble and accepting ... risk takers, really.

The young virgin risked her very life. The Law demanded death for such as she.

The mature carpenter risked his reputation as an honorable man. Association with the young virgin was to publicly declare his guilt.

The weathered shepherds risked more and greater levels of social ostracism.

The well-traveled magi risk the loss of wealth and prestige. Watching stars is one thing but investing time, energy, and money in following them is something else.

The refugee couple risked detection and death.

In our haste to make merry, let us surely remember the Christ child. He must be the focus of our worship and celebration. Yet let us not overlook the angel of the Lord who ignited the spark of wonder and mystery of Christmas, who came into contact with humanity by divine appointment and whispered the glorious news of Christ's advent.

This year may the angel of the Lord find our hearts ready. May we be willing risk takers, too.

Cairo, Egypt
December 1994

Lessons Learned from
the Family Tree

The young boy loved his father's workshop. He loved all the tools. When his father would allow, the boy would carefully (as carefully as a seven-year-old could) handle the wooden mallets and the saws. Often he would reach into the basket where his father kept the wooden pegs that were used for fastening pieces of furniture and equipment together. He would grab a handful of the pegs and line them up in rows of four or five, one row behind the other. Then with a smooth stone he would try to bowl the pegs over. The lad was able to come up with wonderfully creative ideas. He could play for hours with discarded scraps of this and that. But without a doubt, the boy's favorite activity was playing in the pile of wood shavings that his father collected and sold as tinder for cooking fires.

29

On this particular afternoon the son teased his father into wrestling in the shavings. The shavings flew every which way. The two ended in a laughing tangle of elbows and knees. The shavings formed a delightful icing over their sweaty clothes. When finished, they stood and began to shake the shavings back to the floor. The father had shavings throughout his curly black beard. He was a sight to behold. While still flipping shavings from his whiskers, the father reached for the broom. "Daddy," the son asked in a more serious tone, "tell me again about our ancestors."

"Now wait, son. How did you start thinking about our ancestors when we were just wrestling?" the father asked. He waited eagerly for the boy's response. He had learned so much from his son. The lad always had a special way of thinking about things. He was so observant.

The son thought for a moment. "We were wrestling, right?" With a smile the father nodded. "And don't forget that I won," the father teased. The boy laughed and then continued, "We were wrestling in the shavings, right?" "Yes," the father said, still not seeing the connection. "And shavings come from wood which comes from trees, right?" The boy paused long enough to see if his father could make the last connection by himself. When he saw a look of patient puzzlement on his father's face, he completed the thought. "And wood comes from trees and you said the other day that a listing of our ancestors could be called a family…." The father finished the sentence, "*Tree*. Now I get it," he said, shaking his head with a chuckle.

With the last few shavings gathered back into a pile, the father started to speak. "Ancestors … let's see, shall I start way back with Father Adam or shall I just skip to Father Abraham?" The last time the two had had this conversation they had commenced with Adam. It was without a doubt the long version. "Describing a tree by starting with the roots," the father later said when relating the story to the boy's mother. But the last time it was made even longer by the boy's questions. "Where did Cain get his wife?" the boy had interrupted. The father didn't have an answer. "Perhaps you will just have to ask God," he said. The boy was silent for a long time. Finally he spoke. "God created Adam and Eve, right?" The boy began his logical trip. "Yes," the father said. "Well, if God could create Adam and Eve, then I guess he could make a wife for Cain." There was a triumphant finality about the boy's words. It was as if his seven-year old mind had just solved the world's greatest problem and now he was ready to go on to tackle another dilemma. "I'll sleep better tonight knowing that you have discovered the answer to that mystery," the father responded with mock seriousness. Both father and son began to laugh.

"Today give me the quick tour of the family tree, Dad. Start with Abraham," the boy said. The father knew very well that there would be nothing quick about this conversation. The son always asked lots of questions, sometimes questions that forced him to think deeply about his faith and his relationship with God. The boy especially loved the stories of Abraham and King David. He delighted that these two giants of faith were "sitting in the branches of his family tree," as the father put it. "Let's see…. There was Abraham, and then Isaac and…. Who were those guys after Isaac? I can never remember their names." The son was more than ready to complete the list. They had played this game many times before. "Jacob and Judah."

At this point the father interjected the name of Tamar. Later he mentioned Rahab, Ruth, and then Bathsheba. "Father, why did you mention those women in the list?" "You need to know, son, that there are some women up in your tree, too." The boy had never thought about that before; just the way the father said it made the boy giggle.

One by one he asked to hear the stories of these four women. The father was careful not to go into great detail about the questionable lives and practices of some of these women. Yet he told enough. The boy was not shocked, but he was troubled. "You mean we have foreigners, women, and unrighteous people perched in our family tree?" "That is right, son. These we have just been talking about happen to be women. But you need to know that some of the kings in David's line were far from righteous," the father concluded.

The father often wondered, as he saw his son grow older, if that conversation in his workshop had in any way affected his son. It must have. From that day on the boy went out of his way to be kind to foreigners, women, and even the unrighteous.

If the father would have lived long enough, he would have observed his son healing foreigners, valuing women, and welcoming the unrighteous. The father would have also heard from the outwardly religious the jeers that his son touches outcasts, allows women of questionable reputations to approach him, and even eats with sinners. The father would have heard his son say, "I have come not to call the righteous but sinners to repentance."

The father would have been proud.

Cairo, Egypt
December 1994

he young missionary family had been in the Middle East for less than three years. On some days they were amazed to find themselves in this ancient setting. It was like going out your front door and walking into Bible times, except for the traffic, pollution, and noise. They enjoyed their work for the most part. There were many frustrations—language study being chief among them, yet the family had made many friends. Because of the frustrations, there were days when being anyplace else was appealing. Because of the friendships, and, yes, ministry opportunities, they couldn't see themselves anyplace else. In a way they might have been labeled schizophrenic.

One December evening, as the family was getting off the metro at the stop near their home, the speaker system at one of the several mosques in the neighborhood came to life. The father looked at his watch. It wasn't exactly time for the evening call to prayer, but he guessed it was close enough. At intervals during the day and night the *mu'azzin*, or "crier," will sound forth.

> God is great! God is great! God is great! God is great!
> I bear witness that there is no god but God!
> I bear witness that Muhammad is the Apostle of God!
> Come to prayers! Come to prayers!
> Come to salvation! Come to salvation!

The father readied himself for the familiar words. They did not come. Instead, the one holding the microphone began to call upon the name of God. "Allah, Allah, Allah, Allah …" It was like the leader in that particular mosque was holding a special service of intercession and decided to share the service with the community. Again and again he cried out "Allah, Allah, Allah, Allah."

As they walked along, the seven-year old son of the missionary family said, "I know what he is saying, he's saying 'God, God, God.' Why is he saying it over and over again, Daddy?"

"I guess he is praying, son. He wants God to hear his prayers," the father replied, not knowing himself really how to explain the repetition.

As the family walked on, away from the speakers of the mosque, the blaring call of the mosque faded away. The boy's question stayed with the father. "Why are they saying God's name over and over again?"

While tucking his son in bed the missionary father asked him if he knew the word "Emmanuel." "Do you know what it means?" he asked, pulling the covers up around the boy's chin. A smile broke out on the young face. "It means that God is with us."

"That is right, my son," the father continued. "The man at the mosque believes that there is a God. He believes that we can know what God is like. I mean, he thinks people can know that God is strong, generous, and merciful. But he does not know who Jesus is."

The boy looked up at his father and said, "But Dad, the Bible says that Jesus is Emmanuel. If that man knew Jesus, he wouldn't have to keep calling out God's name. He would know that God was with him." As the father left his son's bedside he was humming "O Come, O Come, Emmanuel." He thought of Abraham's prayer for his son, Ishmael, in Genesis. "O that Ishmael might live in your sight!'" He began to sing.

O come, O come, Emmanuel,
And ransom captive *Ishmael*
That mourns in lonely exile here …

O come, Desire of nations,
bind all peoples in one heart and mind;
Bid envy, strife and quarrels cease,
Fill all the world with heaven's peace.

Rejoice! Rejoice! Emmanuel
Shall come to thee, O *Ishmael*.

It was a crazy way to sing the carol. Yet, it truly reflected the heart of the missionary father. As he turned out the hall light that led to his children's bedrooms, the
missionary breathed a prayer for the majority people in the Middle East. He
prayed that Emmanuel would come to ransom the peoples of Ishmael.

Cairo, Egypt
December 1994

The Rumors Are True!

n the small town rumors flew like sparrows. Words whispered in some out-of-the-way spot seemed to take on a life of their own. They winged their way around the community as surely as if an official messenger had assembled all the town's people in the market area and announced a decree of vital importance. The problem with rumors was that they were seldom reliable. Although often there was some small speck of truth at the heart of the rumor, that speck was often chopped, mixed, blended, and baked into an entirely new creation. As a speck of flour is mixed with many ingredients to form a loaf of bread, so, too, with the speck of truth in a rumor. And as with a loaf, many are those who fed on the bread of rumors. As they passed through the lips of persons, one after the other, the stories grew, the misdeed blackened, the offense worsened. No one seemed content to tell the rumor in exactly the same way he had heard it.

There was a certain etiquette in rumor passing and receiving. It was intensely observed in Nazareth. The one passing the rumor would always begin in one of several ways. "I really shouldn't tell you this but …" was in vogue these days. But a rumor could also be identified as such and passed on by saying, "I have it on good authority that …", or simply, "Have you heard that …?"

There was another closely-observed rule in the rumor trade of Nazareth. One never went to the party involved to see if the information being spread had any basis in fact. After all, that might make someone angry. Rumor spreading was safe. It was always secretive. If, when the rumor finally reached the party or parties involved, the persons became angry, well, it was an obvious indication of the truth of the rumor—or so it was believed in Nazareth. Therefore, it was the standard advice of parents to children in Nazareth to try to avoid doing anything that might start a rumor, and if, by chance, a rumor did start about them or their family, try to act like it didn't bother you too much.

Joseph's father was a conscientious man. His carpenter's shop was at the edge of the market area. It was a natural link in the rumor flow of the village. Joseph's father, however, made it clear to his son that he could not stand rumors. He abhorred them. When he himself was young he had been seriously injured by rumors. When someone entered his shop to have some work done—more often than not to just gossip—Joseph's father made it very clear that he had no time for rumors. He took no stock in them. When someone would say, "I really shouldn't tell you this but…" Joseph's father would cut the speaker off in mid-sentence. "If you really shouldn't tell me, don't." That was it. The rumor always had to detour around the carpenter's shop. In other conversations if people strayed into rumors, Joseph's father would quickly and sternly bring the conversation to a close.

Joseph was a keen boy. He watched his father in various settings. He watched how he diplomatically, and on some occasions undiplomatically, handled rumor spreaders. Joseph's father taught his son well. Both by example and specific instruction. "Son, have no part of whisperers." Joseph's father often quoted from Solomon's proverb, "The words of a whisperer are like delicious morsels; they go down into the inner parts of the body." Joseph's father would always add his own wise conclusion to Solomon's saying. "They taste so good going down, but cause the stomach to writhe in pain and must be vomited in order to bring ease." How many times had Joseph heard that advice? Joseph's father always added this admonition to his son, "The best advice I can give you, Joseph, is to always turn the whisperer away at the door. Do not let him spill his poison into your heart and mind."

Joseph was careful to keep his father's advice. And, for the most part, Joseph and his family were not gossiped about or against. They seldom did anything to draw attention to themselves. They were hard working, honest, and circumspect. They were faithful to attend worship at the synagogue in a regular and punctual fashion.

When news of Joseph's engagement to Mary flashed through the town everyone was abuzz. At the well, ladies cooed to one another that they had seen this engagement coming for a long time. "Haven't you seen the way young Joseph has been eyeing Mary?" "And Mary," some other woman responded, "haven't you seen the way she blushes in his presence?" When Mary would come to the well she would receive admiring glances and gentle teasing. Mary's mother was queen of the well for the moment. She would continue to hold this position until the wedding. Although the date had not been officially set, rumor had it that it would be sometime in late spring.

Mary's mother took great pride in her daughter, in her beauty, in her obedience, in her faithfulness, in her purity. Everyone knew that she was Mary's mother. She strutted like a peacock with tail feathers ablaze in glorious color.

How the rumor actually got started no one really knows. Was it a rumor? The grapevine announced in shocked tones that beautiful Mary, pure Mary, was pregnant. The whisperers had a heyday with the story.

Questions about Mary's health were raised by concerned friends. Mary's mother was not seen strutting around the market area. Joseph was turned away from the door when he came to check on his beloved's condition. On the Sabbath Mary's family seemed to shun the young man that they had once welcomed so warmly.

Joseph felt the sting of the rejection, yet he could get no straight answers as to the sudden change in the relationship. He longed to speak to Mary. He needed to hear from her if she had indeed changed her mind about the wedding. To break an engagement, well that was tantamount to divorce. "Why? Why this rejection?" Joseph asked his father in the shop one afternoon.

The elderly carpenter lifted his head from his work. A tear trickled down his cheek and was lost in his graying beard. "Son, when I was about your age I was all set to propose to a young woman. Someone in the town started a rumor about her. The rumor said that she was unfaithful. I believed the rumor and turned my back on her. I never spoke to her again. I discovered later that the story was just a vicious rumor designed to get back at the young woman's family. Her family was forced to leave our village in disgrace. I have regretted my hasty actions all my life and I will carry that regret to my grave." "Son," he continued softly, "the rumors about your young Mary are not good, and you are implicated. Son, rumor has it that your Mary is pregnant and you are the father. Is it true?"

The words hurt as much as if his father had broken a two-by-four over his head. He had seen the looks. He had heard the snickers. He had felt the oppressive weight of untruth building but had no way to identify it. "Mary, pregnant? It could not be! One thing is sure. I am not the father!" He shared none of these thoughts with his father. The pain on Joseph's face, the innocence of his body language, caused Joseph's father to sigh involuntarily.

Now his father spoke again. "Joseph, my son, you must go to Mary. You must discover the truth. You must speak to the one that you love."

Joseph removed his apron slowly and left the shop without further comment. Joseph soundlessly opened the door, exited, and closed it behind him. Joseph's pain was obvious. Joseph's father latched the door and then walked to the old cane chair in the corner of the room. He sat down heavily and tried to pray for his boy. But even as he did the pain of his past caved in upon him. He cried like a baby.

Joseph walked to Mary's house. It was a path that he had so often traveled with joy. He knew each rock, bend, and tree. This evening he noticed nothing. He walked as in a daze. He longed to be at Mary's house, yet he dreaded being there at the same time. What would he say? How would he convince Mary's parents to let him see her? And then he was at the door. Mary's father answered the door. "You are not welcome here," he spoke the words with deathly finality.

"Please, sir, I must see Mary," Joseph pleaded. "I must talk to her. I must—I must ask her," his words trailed off.

"About the rumors?" Mary's father stormed. "The rumors are true! How could you disgrace my family like this? How could you disgrace your family?!" The door slammed in a resounding thud. The whole wall of the house shook.

Joseph heard Mary sobbing in her room. "Let me speak to him, Papa, please. It is not what you think." "NO!" came the thundering reply.

"The rumors are true. The rumors are true." The words spun in his mind as Joseph retraced his steps toward home. Some place along that path Joseph made up his mind to divorce Mary. Oh how he loved her. He would never publicly charge her or embarrass her. But he was certain that he could not go through with the marriage. It was over.

In the darkness of his room, Joseph poured out his heart to God. "Is there anything that can take away the pain I feel? Can anyone replace the void I have in my heart?" The questions were rhetorical. The answer Joseph expected to hear from God was silence, a loud silent confirmation saying, "There is nothing to ease your pain, nothing to fill the void." However, in his moment of turmoil an angel spoke to him.

"Joseph," his name was spoken in comforting tones, "do not be afraid to take Mary as your wife. The child within her is not from some other man. How could that be? Mary loves only you. She would never do anything to harm you. No, the child within her is from God." As simply as possible the angel explained to Joseph God's plan. The angel continued, "When it is time, Mary will give birth to a son and you will give him the name *Jesus* because he will save his people from their sins."

"The Messiah?" Joseph breathed.

"Yes, my child, the Messiah."

Joseph's mind darted to the passage he had been meditating on just prior to all the rumors ... rather, the truth. "Behold a virgin shall conceive and bear a son and he will be called Immanuel."

"Mary's child is *Immanuel*?"

The angel smiled the smile of a teacher who has finally seen the light in the student's eyes after explaining a difficult concept.

Joseph's countenance darkened. "What about Mary's parents? What about the people in Nazareth? What about the rumors?"

"Do you remember the stories of Moses?" the angel asked. Of course Joseph did. Every child in Israel knew those stories. "God will prepare the path for you through the sea. Be faithful to walk." The angel vanished.

The restlessness and turmoil were gone. It had been replaced with a holy expectancy. "Mary's child is the Messiah. Jesus. Immanuel. Be faithful to walk."

And in those moments following the angel's departure Joseph made a vow before his God to love and cherish Mary, to care for the child, and to be faithful to walk when and where God opened the door.

Cairo, Egypt
November 1994

"hy have you have disgraced us like this?" The words were more accusation than question. In the room the atmosphere was highly charged. Her father marched around the confined space like a general. At one point, his emotions rising to a fever pitch, he picked up a wooden bucket and flung it against the stone wall of the crude dwelling. Splinters showered the room. Pain and anger drove him nearly mad. Lightening shot from his eyes, thunder rumbled in his voice. "Why?!" was the only question that was spoken. Again the question. "Why?" His voice began to shake, his energy spent, he crumpled to the floor, mumbling "Why? Why?" Off in the corner the mother who had moved to protect her daughter from the threat of violence heaved a heavy sigh and began to cry silently. Tears coursed their way down her broad weather-beaten face cascading off her nose and landing silently on the hay-covered floor. Mary now moved to embrace her protector. "Why won't you believe me?" Her voice pleaded. Her mother's response was full of pain, "Your story is simply too incredible, my child."

Earlier that same day Mary had spoken with Yousef, her intended. She told him about the angel, the message, her question of how this could be possible because she wasn't married. She relayed the angel's answer and how she had found abiding peace and assurance that everything would be just as the angel said. More importantly, she expressed of her belief that everything would be all right. Yousef had listened incredulously and then heavily, painfully, slowly turned and walked away without so much as a word.

A child of thirteen can only handle so much rejection and trauma in one day. From her father's boisterous, blasting charge that she had disgraced her family, to the tearful lack of trust of her mother, to the silent pain of her fiancé; it was almost too much. Almost. Somehow in the midst of all the trauma of the day she slept peacefully. For her the firm conviction "with God all things are possible" was enough. Still she wondered why God had chosen her to carry his Son.

Such was not the case for her fiancé. Yousef tossed and turned. He cried out to God in fervent prayer. He railed against his fate. He demanded answers to questions that he couldn't even form in his troubled mind. The only question that forced its way to his lips was "Why, God, *why?*" Anxious and distraught, he determined to divorce Mary. She deserved to die, so said the Law. But he could never bring himself to fulfill the letter of the Law. In the midst of this turmoil he slept. As he slept he found comfort and answers.

The vision was so real, so tangible. The angel was at his bedside. The holiness of that angel was so evident. "I have come from God on high to speak to your pain and grief. I have come to both comfort and command you. What Mary says is true. She is carrying God's own Son. Take her as your wife. Love her and protect her. Love and protect the child for the child within her will save his people from their sins." Yousef awoke still feeling the warmth of his heavenly visitor. The awful weight of doubt and depression had lifted. Joy replaced sadness. Faith took up residence in his soul. He believed. In the darkness of his room he made plans to speak to Mary, her family, and his own family.

When he approached Mary's small house, he was treated coldly. Mary's mother made it very clear that Yousef was fortunate that Mary's father was not home. "He is threatening to tear you limb from limb," she said forcefully. "Leave us alone. Haven't you caused us enough pain?"

As Mary's mother turned to enter the house, Mary was standing in the doorway. All she heard was Yousef's words, "I believe you, Mary" and all she saw was a fleeting glance of his peaceful face. It was enough. Of course all this happened in the tiniest fraction of a second for Mary's mother roughly shoved her daughter inside, shouting over her shoulder, "And don't come back, Yousef Ben Yacoub!"

Yousef should have been disheartened, but he was not. Faith and hope bubbled within him like two fresh water springs on the edge of a rocky and barren wilderness. He determined to speak to his family.

"Why have you disgraced this family?" his mother screeched. "Why could you not have waited." It was like his parents had heard nothing of what he had said about the visitation to Mary and his own vision of confirmation. "What do you take us for, fools?" His mother ranted on. "And if we won't accept this make-believe story, how do you think our neighbors will ever believe?"

Yousef's father was silent, much like Yousef had been upon hearing Mary's account. He needed time to think. Without so much as a word Yousef's father grabbed his garment from the peg near the door and slowly walked out onto the dusty lane. The weight of the world rested squarely on his shoulders. Yousef was quick to follow.

They walked along in silence, these two men who were so much alike. The first word that Yousef's father spoke was "Why?" It wasn't a question that demanded an answer. Outside of the village Yousef's father spoke again. "You must marry her, my son."

"Do you believe me? Do you believe Mary? Do you believe us?" Yousef cried out.

"Your story is too incredible. I know what God's word says about a Messiah. But why us? Why our family? Why the disgrace?" The questions tumbled out in rapid succession. And then a long pause. "But this I know," he continued. "We are a family that does what is right regardless of the cost." Yousef's father again plunged into silence. The silence between father and son was as thick as the dust on the road. And then Yousef's father asked what he thought were the two most important questions. "Do you believe Mary, my son, and do you still love her?" With Yousef's affirmative answers to both questions his father determinedly turned back toward the village and went to the home of Mary.

Anger, recrimination, and hostility had taken up residence in the home of Mary. Plans were already underway to send Mary off to her cousin's house outside of Jerusalem. It was clearly a face-saving move, an attempt to do something until something better could be thought of.

Mary, according to her father, was "damaged goods." Yousef, according to his mother, was an unfaithful, ungrateful son. Finally let's-make-the-best-out-of-the-worst-situation negotiations were made and by the end of the week a "quiet" marriage was arranged. Of course nothing was quiet in this village. What people didn't know, they suspected.

In time all the village suspicions became clearly evident. Mary was pregnant. This was the reason for the rushed marriage. This was why the families had no joy in the union of their children. This was why mothers were not boasting and clucking proudly about their children. This was why Yousef took his child-bride away to Bethlehem to give birth to their son who was so unfortunate to be conceived outside the bonds of marriage. Never mind that Yousef had taxes to pay. Everyone in that village believed it was a ruse.

What Mary and Yousef knew and believed was not shared by their families or their neighbors. They knew Jesus was not given to disgrace them, their families, or even their village. God had given Jesus to bless, not disgrace. They knew that he was given to save his people from their sins. They knew that this tiny infant would somehow turn the world upside down.

· · · · ·

One evening as Yousef cradled the infant Jesus in his arms, marveling over his beauty and perfection, the uncertainty of the future of his little family flooded over him. "Why, God, have you enfolded us into your plans? Why us? And why won't our families believe? Why won't they accept this tiny boy as your Son?" As he settled the infant in the feeding trough Mary came and placed her hand on his shoulder. She had seen the questions churning in her beloved's eyes. She knew his heart. She felt his concern. Yet she spoke words of faith. "For us these things are impossible to understand, my husband. But remember that with God all things are possible." Yousef embraced his wife and whispered his love for her and the child into her long dark hair.

Then they slept.

Again Yousef had a vision. Again a visitation. Again a command. "Take the child and flee." And they did. Neither he nor Mary stopped to ask why.

Beirut International Church, Lebanon
December 2000

Emmanuel's Labor

anks' Book Nook was located at the corner of sixth and Main—just down from a Big Boy's Restaurant and Watsons', an old "five and dime." Just across the street was a men's clothing store. On the corner of Seventh and Main was a music store, a sporting goods store, and The Paramount, the one theater in town, and the Readi-Cab office. Off Main Street a block or two was the local Y.M.C.A., and diagonally across the street from the "Y" was the large limestone edifice of the First Presbyterian Church. George was an active member in both the "Y" and the church. Main Street was a good location for the store. It was in the heart of the town's business district.

George Banks, the owner of The Book Nook, had been in business in Madison for almost thirty years. Over that length of time George and his wife, Myrna, had built up a sizeable equity in the store. Just last year George and Myrna had received the local Chamber of Commerce's Award for Excellence and Integrity in business. George was justly proud of the recognition. The plaque hung just to the right side of his cash register.

George had completed only a sixth grade education. On Thanksgiving Day of George's seventh-grade year his father had suffered a heart attack. He lingered for a week or so, and then, in early December, died. As the oldest son, George felt it was necessary to leave school to take a job in order to help support his family. George had seen many hard times. That he was successful at all was a minor miracle. Of course George did not view it that way. George was proud of his success. He attributed it to hard work and faith in God. When given the opportunity, he could wax eloquently about the merits of both work and faith, although to be honest, George really leaned heavily on the hard work side, and then coated his comments with a decorative covering of faith. Often his words about work were cold and hard, like frozen ground. The faith part was the wispy snow that was scattered here and there to give the wintry words a Christmas card appearance. Bluntly, George was the kind of man who had little patience with the poor. He called them "freeloaders." Anyone on welfare, anyone who received food stamps, anyone who came to the food pantry at his church, well—they needed to get to work, reach down, and pull themselves up by their own bootstraps, quit looking for handouts, and in the process, find some faith in the "man upstairs." When George talked like this Myrna would shiver. She had long ago given up trying to change her husband. She loved him in spite of his frosty work ethic.

George had started selling newspapers, magazines, books—paperbacks mostly—and cards. Myrna was kind of a "crafty" lady, so when the store opened up next door they expanded the business to include craft supplies, candles, quilts on consignment, knickknacks, and seasonal items.

George loved the Christmas season. He enjoyed playing Christmas music in his store, often he sang along with his rich bass voice. He liked decorating with holly and mistletoe. He enjoyed saying "Ho! Ho! Ho! Merry Christmas!" when people would leave his store. He liked to hear Christmas bells ringing. He always asked the Salvation Army to put one of their kettles in front of his store. He liked the sound of those ringing bells outside. That the Salvation Army kettle outside his door brought him more customers didn't bother him either. George often joked at the Chamber of Commerce meetings that he was partial to the bells of Christmas, particularly the ringing bells of his cash register. That line always got him a laugh.

Now don't get me wrong. George was no Scrooge. He was careful to tithe, although going beyond a tithe was a bit troublesome for him. Once Myrna had given a generous offering for missions after a Presbyterian missionary working with tribal peoples in Indonesia had come through. George was not angry, and he didn't begrudge the missionary the necessary funds to carry on his work. "After all," he said, "those heathen over there need to get a little faith." What did anger George was, as he put it, "the pew sitters in our church who didn't pay even a tithe. Why, if everyone would just pay their tithe, missionaries wouldn't have any need to come around asking for more money. There would be more than enough money to win the world twice over!" In George's logic, God had asked him to give ten percent of his income. (George even gave ten percent of his gross income.) God trusted George with the remaining ninety percent. "If I am careful and invest my ninety percent wisely," George went on expansively, "there will be a bigger ten percent for God next year!"

The aroma in the shop was wonderful. It was a mixture of bayberry candles and white chocolate. Christmas carols were playing softly in the background. Myrna had made Santa hats for herself and George. Myrna was in the back room wrapping a Christmas gift for a customer—it was a free service they provided. George was moving a heavy cardboard carton of Thanksgiving cards from the front of the store into storage. A pain shot through his chest and down his arm. He dropped the box. Cards scattered every which way. The customer and Myrna rushed to George's side. George's pulse was racing. He was nauseous. His skin color took on a grayish hue. It was obvious he was having a heart attack. Myrna began to weep. The customer ran for the phone. Soon the Christmas atmosphere was cut by the wail of the siren.

Unstable for almost a week, George was hooked up to all kinds of machines in the Coronary Care Unit. Finally George was released to a coronary ward and now came tests and more tests to determine the extent of the damage to the heart itself. The prognosis was not good. More than forty-percent of his heart muscle had been deadened. The doctor informed George that heart muscle does not repair itself.

When George was not sleeping his mind would return to his seventh-grade year, the year when his father had died of a heart attack. Sometimes big tears would splash on his hospital pajamas. "God, I don't want to die yet," George would pray.

Around five A.M. each morning Steve Wilson would come by to visit George. George had known Steve since Steve was in diapers. Steve and his parents attended the Presbyterian Church with George. Steve was a morning blood drawer. He didn't always take blood from George; sometimes Steve just showed up to talk, read Scripture, and pray. George became impressed with the vibrant faith of this young man.

As Christmas Day approached many people were discharged from the hospital. Yet George was forced to remain. He was agitated by his doctor's firmness on the issue.

The day before Christmas Steve showed up at George's bedside. George had taken a turn for the worse. Steve could see the difference in his friend. Steve did as he was in the habit of doing. He pulled out his Bible and read to George. George asked to hear the Christmas story. Steve began in Matthew, intending to read the Luke account, as well.

Steve read the part about Jesus coming to forgive people their sins and also that Jesus was to be called Emmanuel, "God with us." George reached out his hand and stopped his young friend. "You know," he said, "I have heard that passage all my life but somehow it has never struck me. I want to know that my sins are forgiven. I have worked all my life to somehow prove to God that I was good enough." George smiled as a thought came to him. "Maybe I have been so intent on the necessity of manual labor to reach heaven that I overlooked Emmanuel's labor."

"Read me the story of the cross, Steve." Steve read from Luke this time. When Steve read the words of Jesus, "Father, forgive them; for they do not know what they are doing," George stopped Steve again. "I need to know that I am forgiven, Steve. Is it possible that I can be absolutely sure?" Steve faithfully shared the gospel and George tearfully accepted Emmanuel's labor and gave up on his own.

Steve was off for Christmas Day. Before leaving George's bedside the day before he had promised to return to visit his friend on the twenty-sixth, but George Banks died on Christmas day in the arms of his wife. His last words to Myrna were "Find Steve Wilson and tell him I'm trusting solely in Emmanuel's labor."

Cairo, Egypt
December 1994

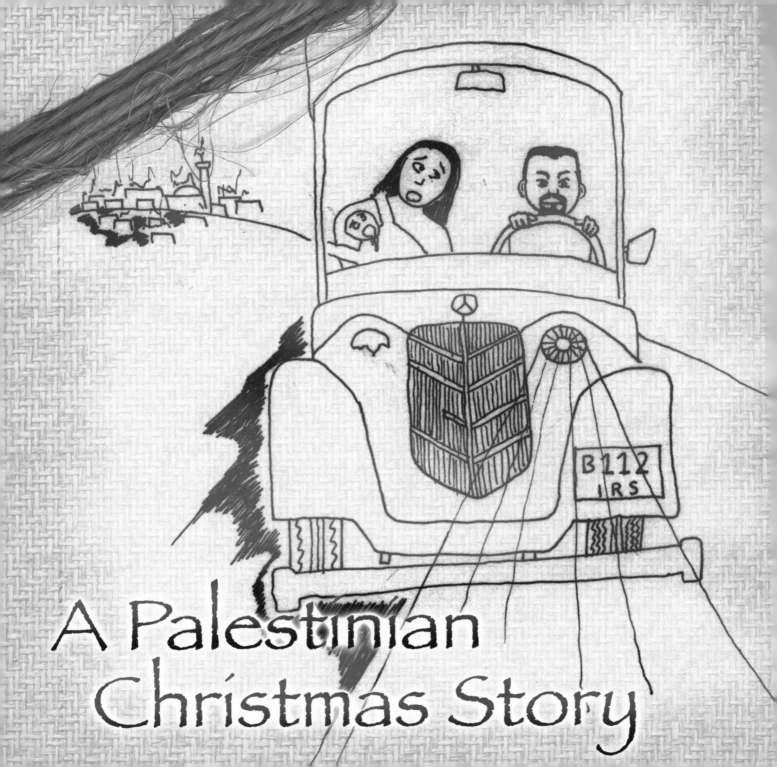

A Palestinian
Christmas Story

They were refugees. They were fugitives. When they left they were unable to carry much with them. A few belongings: a raggedy leather suitcase, a change of clothes, a few tins of unlabeled food, a small stack of *baladi* bread. In one carry-on-type bag with a broken strap they had some baby stuff. Deep inside the carry-on were stuffed three recently received gifts. This small family felt like pieces of wood tossed recklessly down a swollen stream. Things seemed out of control.

Panic flashed in her eyes. The question "What if they catch us?" formed on her tongue, but was left unspoken. Her heart beat wildly, a pace almost double the cadence of the old car's windshield wipers. One headlight was out. The mother worried that the headlight might be a reason to be stopped by the security police. The father struggled to see the roadway. In a land where it seldom rained, when it did it was like the skies were trying to make up for lost time.

Now was such a time.

The heater in the old car with balding tires was on-again-off-again. At this moment it was off. The mother tucked a woolen blanket around her tired child. The boy shivered. The mother spoke words of calm to the child, words she herself didn't quite believe. She wondered if her toddler was already able to sense her tension and fear. From the look in the child's eyes and the strength of his grip as he squeezed her fingers, she guessed that the youngster was well aware of the situation, maybe not the details, but certainly the urgency. She smiled down at her boy. Never a cry of complaint, nary a whimper. She hugged him close to her breast.

She looked over at her husband. He was hunched over the steering wheel. His clothes were very worn. Concern, determination and confidence—all three were engraved on his face. It was a strange mixture; strange, that is, for anyone except her husband. She knew him well and loved him. Those calloused hands and strong arms. She longed that he would pull the car to the side of the road and just hug her and the child, to calm her fears. She said nothing.

He skillfully navigated the one-eyed car down out of the hill country. He neatly avoided the checkpoints. If he could just make it to Gaza. The blue tags on his uncle's car clearly indicated their origin. A large white "B" was stamped on the plate. The "B" told all that the car was registered in Bethlehem and that the passengers were Palestinians.

As fatigue crashed upon the driver he thought back to the night when, in a dream, the angel had spoken to him. "Do not be afraid to take Mary as your wife. She is pregnant. But God is the father." He thought of all the

53

shame he had endured by identifying with the young woman sitting by his side. When the knowledge of her pregnancy ricocheted throughout Bethlehem, the young couple faced great persecution. Even these days Palestinian families sometimes murdered girls who got pregnant out of wedlock. He clung to those words, "Do not be afraid."

When the small family did pause to rest, the father heard the same words over and over again. "Get up! Hurry and take the child and his mother to Egypt! Stay there until I tell you to return, because Rothman is looking for the child and wants to kill him."

Elias Rothman was the newly-elected Prime Minister in Israel. He was a non-practicing Jew. Religion for him was a sham. Of course, from time to time he made religious-sounding speeches and made appearances at religious events. But it was for show. He was a politician first and foremost. Everything was said and done to garner votes, to impress the electorate. He was cruel and ruthless, cold and calculating. Winning and power were everything. How had this insignificant couple from outside of Bethlehem caught the attention of the Rothman government? On the very day when the Israeli government was signing a peace accord with Jordan and working on secret peace negotiations with Syria and Lebanon, two scientists and one important Rabbi from Eastern Europe had flown into Ben Gurion Airport. Because of the Rabbi's connections within the Hasidic community, he was able to obtain an audience with Rothman himself.

Rothman was a no-nonsense sort of man. He was not one to waste time with pleasantries. He cut through all the nice talk with somewhat brusque words. "Rabbi, with all due respect, I'm a busy man. You, too, must be busy. Please come to the point."

"Prime Minister Rothman, my associates and I are convinced that the Messiah has come." The words caught Rothman off guard. The Rabbi spoke with such conviction. A pulse of fright. The Rabbi plunged on. "We have seen a star rising in the heavens. We are convinced that this is a sign, a declaration from God himself that the time has come."

The conversation, and subsequent ones, convinced Rothman that these men were not religious fanatics. He had to take their words seriously. After all, he himself had gone out the past several nights and witnessed the star. It was magnificent. It was comet-like but stationary over Jerusalem.

The three visitors were given a government Mercedes to travel the last seven miles to Bethlehem. The driver was told to do exactly as the visitors requested. They left Jerusalem at 8:30 P.M. As closely as possible they "followed" the star. Really they didn't follow the star, for it scarcely moved. Yet the light of the star seemed to focus into a beam. In a miraculous way the starlight seemed to shine brightly on a smallish house on the road down

out of Bethlehem on the way to The Shepherds Field. It was the family home of the refugee father.
The driver of the car, himself a captain in the security forces, was asked to wait outside. As he did he radioed in the exact location of the house in the Occupied Territories. The security police were alerted, but on Rothman's orders, didn't move in.

When the Rabbi and the two believing scientists entered the home, they bowed and worshiped the child. Although they could not speak the same language, they made two things very clear. They believed the child was the Messiah, and they wanted to give this new king gifts. They opened their luggage and removed the lining. They gave the father $3,000 in U.S. currency, some expensive aromatic spices, and a coarsely made wooden cross.

The visitors departed the room, breathing a collective prayer for the safety of the child. They were worried about what Rothman might try. Before leaving they had spoken very briefly about their concern. Never in their wildest dreams did they believe that the new Israeli Prime Minister intended on abducting and then getting rid of this kingly child.

Undercover security forces, however, were, at that very moment, encircling that section of Bethlehem. They had been instructed to wait until the visitors had left and then close in and "detain" the child and his parents.

As the mother put the child to bed, in another room the father fell into a heavy sleep. He had no idea how long he slept. While he slept the angel spoke. He woke instantly. Moving quickly and quietly about the small room the father gathered their few possessions, and stuffed them into their second hand luggage. Only when the two bags were packed did he go into the room where the mother and child were. He whispered to the mother, "An angel just spoke to me. The visitors were right. We must leave right now."

His wife was startled. "Can't we say good-bye to our family?"

The father was already out the door, sleeping child in his arms. "No time," was all he said. The mother grabbed her wrap and obediently followed.

The car made its customary grinding sound before starting and, finally, coughed to life. They were off. How they were able to clear out unnoticed was a miracle. The security police informed Rothman that it was not possible for anyone to have left undetected. This overconfidence on the part of the police bought the small family much needed time.

Rothman, believing that the family was trapped in an ever-tightening net, issued orders for a house-to-house search. Then he slept confidently. He believed that by the first light of morning this "threat to national security," as he had described it, would be taken care of. Yet, in the morning, as the family was crossing the Rapha border under the amazing protection of God's hand, Rothman was cursing his incompetent security chief.

The Jerusalem Post detailed the tragic fire that occurred just outside of Bethlehem. The paper said that many young children were killed in the blaze. "It was a tragedy of international proportions," the paper reported. As to the cause of the blaze, arson was suspected. News of the police search and threat to national security never made it into the paper. Those things were often rumored but the government always kept a tight rein on the press.

On the night of the escape into Egypt, the father knew none of the details. What he did know was that his family was in danger. Father, mother, and son dropped into a restless sleep on the bus ride to Cairo. They did not even notice the Coptic Orthodox nun sitting across the aisle. When they crossed the Suez Canal the father awoke. The sister was so friendly. It wasn't long before the father and the Coptic nun were engaged in a conversation.

The boy's father found out that the nun, Sister Mona, was from Assuit. She lived in Durunka Convent in the mountains just south of the city. The nun found out that this family had just arrived from Bethlehem. She discovered that the father was a carver, a craftsman. In passing, Sister Mona invited the family to come to Assuit to visit her. At that moment the toddler stirred. The conversation ended. Once in Cairo the father was still uncomfortable, uneasy. He decided to push ahead. "Where will we go?" asked the tired mother. "Assuit," he responded without even thinking. They cashed a bit of their money and caught a train from the Ramses station. Seven hours later they pulled into Assuit.

Assuit was like a city under siege. The police in that area were engaged in a constant battle with Muslim extremists. Armed police were everywhere. The presence of the police made the father nervous. He quickly flagged a rumpled service taxi for the trip to the convent.

The taxi driver was a rough-looking, heavyset man. He was unfriendly. When he learned that he had to travel outside the city, he became more so. For a moment he thought of turning down the fare. He needed the money though. His family had to eat. His children needed clothes. He waved to the family to get in.

The air in Assuit was very cool, cold really. The windows of the taxi were tightly shut except for the driver's side. That window was partially open so that the driver's cigarette smoke could escape. The taxi was so beaten down that it almost didn't make it up the hill to the convent. With steam belching out of the radiator, the car pulled to a stop outside the gate of the convent.

Somehow, just being in the presence of this tired and frightened-looking family softened the Muslim driver. About halfway out of town he had ground his cigarette into a crumpled stub. He apologized for the smoke. Looking in his rearview mirror he saw the mother and child. He smiled for the first time on the journey, the first time all day. Even though his car had labored badly to make the trip, upon arrival the driver would take nothing for his services. It was strange. No meaningful conversation passed between the driver and the family, yet the driver had been changed. As he related the story later to his family, he said, "I couldn't take any money for the trip. I received something unspeakable just by offering my service to the child and his family." He rambled on, "It was like being in the presence of one of God's prophets. No, on second thought, it was like being in the presence of our God himself, but …" his voice trailed off in wonder, "and he is love." The words amazed him and his family.

At the convent, the family was quickly put in touch with Sister Mona. She provided lodging for the tired travelers. Later she arranged for work for the father. He became the convent's carpenter and handyman.

The family stayed at the convent for several years. Miraculous things seemed to happen around the child, inexplicable things. The most amazing thing that happened was when Sister Mona fell ill. She was diagnosed with cancer of the spine. Several weeks after the diagnosis, with sister Mona growing weaker and weaker, the fast-growing cancer spreading unchecked throughout her body, the child prayed a simple prayer at bedtime. "Daddy," he prayed according to his usual fashion, "Auntie Mona needs your help. Please remember how much she has helped us. Amen." At the conclusion of his prayer he announced to his parents that his heavenly Father had heard the prayer and would answer.

The next morning when the father was heading to his workshop he saw Mona. She was heading to Mass. Her once-ashen face was fresh and alive. Her once crumpled form was straight. Not only was she walking, there was a noticeable spring in her step, bu. praises were also on her lips. All morning long the father pondered the miracle. At lunch he related the incident to his family. "Why are you so surprised, my father? Didn't I tell you that God had answered my prayers?"

Al Ahram and other newspapers in Egypt were full of announcements of the sudden death of the Israeli Prime Minister Elias Rothman. That very night the father had a dream. The angel said it was now safe to return to Israel. Sister Mona, through connections, was able to secure the proper paperwork for the family. This time when they traveled across the Rapha border, they faced no difficulties.

They returned and lived in Nazareth. The father began to work in the area as a handyman-carpenter. The mother bore other children and carried on the household. The son grew strong and tall. He pleased his parents, and was always kind and helpful to others. Without a doubt he pleased God, too.

Cairo, Egypt
November 1994

Iraq

Iraqi Mystics
Follow the Star

With the naked eye they scanned the heavens, these magi, these non-professional Iraqi astrologers. These were mystics, not scientists.

Most in the scientific community in Iraq were in the government employ. Therefore, by government decree, they were forced to concentrate on one of two essential matters—oil or expansion. The oil forced the scientific community to look down, to examine rock formations, soil consistency; often, in this scientific age, the scientists poured over satellite images for telltale signs of natural deposits of petroleum. With enough oil Iraq could control the economies of their neighbors—friends and enemies alike.

Military expansion was the other great aim of the Iraqi leadership. There was an intense "mobilization of science," as the government labeled it, to provide adequate weaponry to become the dominant power in the whole region. Years of war with Iran, followed by a shattering setback during the Gulf War, had not deterred the Iraqi leadership from the necessity of military development and expansion. This goal of expansion forced the scientists to follow the gaze of the leadership into the backyards of their neighbors and to bring to reality the dream equipment necessary to stage a victorious military campaign.

These mystical, non-professional sky-gazers were unfettered by dreams of economic control and imperialistic conquest. They studied the skies for some sign from God himself. They were firmly convinced that God wanted to communicate with humanity, that God was interested in the right of all to fellowship with himself and in right relationship with others. They were longing for God himself to enter in on the side of those who seek God. The government announced that God was on the side of those who battled for God against the infidel; that is, anyone who opposed their "divinely appointed right to rule." There was little that was religious about the government's attitude and actions. Power was what they sought. Power came dressed in many outfits: economic planner, religious fanatic, and military strategist. No, the mystical astrologers were not like these at all.

It should be no surprise that when God set his star blazing in the heavens, only the mystics saw *and* understood. They were able to focus and comprehend, not because they had keener physical eyesight than the others in Iraq. They saw with eyes that had been trained on seeking after God.

Somehow these five mystics understood that they must follow this star. In a world of exit permits and entry visas, it was no small task. They applied in various offices, they stood in long lines, underwent intense interrogation. Yet nothing would deter them from their goal. When asked why they wanted to leave their country they simply responded, "Religious Pilgrimage." Pilgrimage was a concept well-known in the area. When they had completed all the screening, however, only three of the five mystics were permitted to leave. No reason was given for the rejection of the two, but then governments such as this one need not provide reasons.

The mystics determined to go to Jerusalem as it was a place of holy pilgrimage for them. When they arrived they were detained for two days by Israeli security guards. It seemed likely that they would not be allowed to enter. Yet, miraculously, clearance came from somewhere up the chain of command. The mystics knew why they had been allowed entry—"the hand of God."

They cleared customs and headed directly for the Knesset, the Israeli parliament. But they should have known that governments and mystics have little in common. They found no one but bureaucrats interested in water rights and religious fanaticism. No one gave them the time of day.

They headed for Gaza. Surely someone there would know. The star was so visible. "Why can't people see it?" they wondered. In Gaza they found political maneuvering and even bloodshed. They realized that they were no closer to an end to their quest here than they had been in Baghdad or Jerusalem. Dejectedly they headed for home. Their religious pilgrimage had turned into a religious hoax. Yet in the heavens the star burned even more brightly.

In a news stand in Jerusalem they saw a reference to a star in the heavens. They grasped each other by the shoulders and danced with delight. Finally someone had seen what they had been following. They purchased the paper. It turned out to be a scientific report. Their mystic hearts bottomed out.

A group of Palestinian school children passed the three men. They spoke in excited tones about a star. Near the Dome of the Rock they witnessed a small cluster of Jewish schoolboys pointing to "their" star and talking with great animation.

A Palestinian shopkeeper served as translator. All the schoolboys except one fled the scene. What if someone saw them talking with these foreign Arabs? The one remaining boy was very nervous at first. He answered the questions in a perfunctory manner. Yet he was won over by the keen interest of the mystics in what he referred to as "his" star. He had seen it every night for several months. Some children his age had seen it. No adult seemed to see it.

The boy spoke of Bethlehem. The shopkeeper closed his shop and said he would be happy to take the mystics to Bethlehem. They invited the boy to join them, but that was just too much. They agreed that the schoolboy should come by the shop the next day. If the shopkeeper had any news, he would pass it on to the lad.

The shopkeeper dressed the mystics as Palestinian Arabs. They wore checkered *kefayahs* (scarfs) and jackets and jeans. It certainly wasn't the wardrobe of a mystic where they came from. They accepted the change of clothing, nonetheless.

The old battered Peugeot headed out of the city. How they cleared the checkpoint is impossible to describe. At one point Israeli security forces were checking the driver's ID and getting ready to ask the three in the backseat for their papers and then he was flagging them through.

The driver shook his head and laughed. The mystics had seen enough of these seeming miracles on this trip. They simply smiled, smiles of faith.

What the mystics did not know was that the security personnel at the Knesset had received reports of the foreign Arab men bothering people in front of the building. A search had been made of all entry records. The computer mistake was found. An all-points bulletin was out on these men. They were wanted for questioning and then deportation.

The night had been dark and overcast. They couldn't see anything in the heavens. Was this a sign that they were on the wrong track? They decided that they would drive up and down the hills of Bethlehem until they received some sign. The driver was skeptical, but it was more interesting than sitting in his shop trying to sell souvenirs to non-existent tourists. Two of the mystics searched the heavens and the third prayed that God would reveal to them divine direction.

And it did come. The clouds parted and starlight streamed through the opening. The light clearly rained from heaven on one particular area of the city. As they neared that place, they realized that the light was even more localized. One small house was illuminated in the inky blackness.

The men were thrilled. Their pilgrimage was nearing an end. They entered the house and found Mary, Joseph, and a toddler. They worshiped the child and gave him gifts worthy of a king. Their joy was uncontained. They felt as if they had found the love of God. Yet, even for their mystical minds, it was hard to grasp how all that love could be packaged in the body of a toddler.

Back at the house of the shopkeeper, the mystics were warned in a dream not to try to leave Israel via the airport. Instead, with the help of the shopkeeper, they were able to be smuggled out of the country by ship from the port of Haifa.

The next afternoon around four o'clock the Jewish schoolboy showed up. The shopkeeper's store was closed. For several days the boy continued to pass by the shop. The heavy metal, pull-down shutters were tightly sealed. Each night the sky was the same, dark and overcast. No moon and no stars, no star. The boy began to lose hope. On the fifth day, the boy's mystical heart sagging like a well-used gate, he saw that the store was no longer shuttered. He ran up the alley, found the shopkeeper, and heard the marvelous story. His mystical heart soared to new heights.

There on a cobblestone street, as dusk descended, a Palestinian shopkeeper and an Israeli schoolboy celebrated the arrival of the Messiah. And the Iraqi astrologers-mystics? They returned home and spread the news about the child of peace and love that they had found by following the star.

Cairo, Egypt
December 1994

61

Stories Woven From Luke's Threads

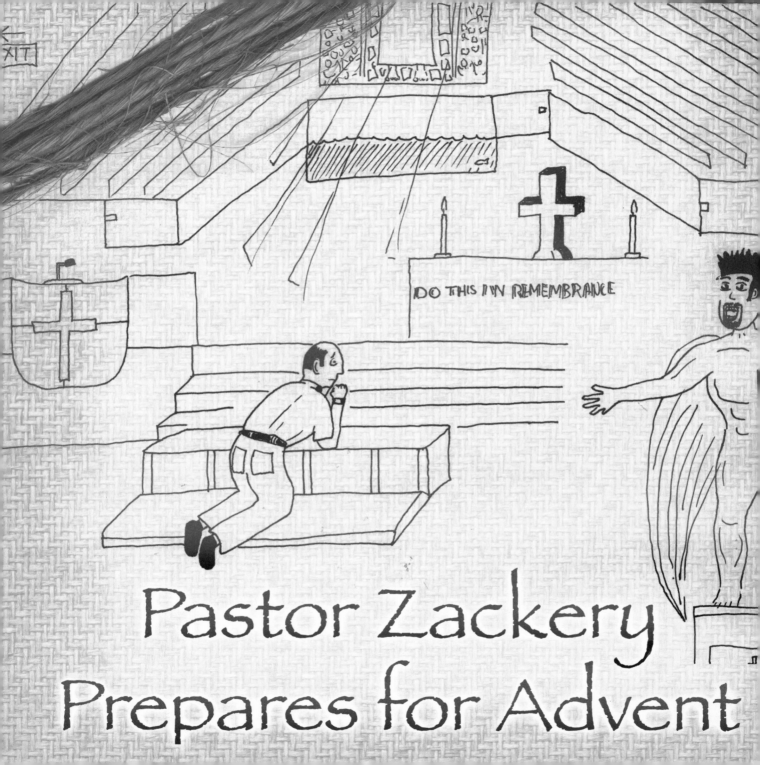

DO THIS IN REMEMBRANCE

Pastor Zackery
Prepares for Advent

Although his church was not the biggest in the city, Fairfield Methodist Church was not the smallest either. Rev. Zackery Priest was fifty-six years old and had pastored in several locations, all in the Northeast. His present pastorate was stressful. He had a very intellectual congregation. He spent hours and hours each week on his knees and at his desk trying to prepare sermons that equipped, challenged, and inspired his people. Most of the time he was long on equipment and short on challenge and inspiration. He felt more like a quartermaster handing out shovels and rakes than like a gardener cooperating with the Creator to fashion these people into a beautiful masterpiece. In moments of honest introspection, he realized that he should never have accepted this pulpit. He simply wasn't cutting it. After five dry years he was beginning to think about moving on. Maybe he should consider leaving the ministry. Many of the people he had studied with in seminary had already left. But Pastor Zackery couldn't do that. His age was against such a move. He knew that if he left Fairfield he only had one good pastorate in front of him. He had talked with his District Superintendent and had asked to be relocated. "A smaller, slower-paced, simpler body of believers" was what he had requested. The D.S. understood.

Pastor Zackery always tried to put his best foot forward during the Advent Season. He began planning these sermons in mid-October. He lived with them a long time. His people always recognized the quality of these messages. A matronly lady in his congregation once commented when "passing in review" of the pastor after an Advent service two years back, "why can't all your sermons be as good as this one?" It was a back-handed compliment to be sure. What Pastor Zackery thought, but did not say, was, "I'm always having to run around putting out fires, doing work that God's people should be doing, cleaning bathrooms, picking up bulletins after the service, answering the telephone, and so on."

It was late October. The large silver maple on the front lawn of the church was in glorious color. "Oh, that my sermons would reflect the glory of God like that maple." He was brought back to reality by the phone. His secretary was gone on a pregnancy leave. The ringing phone reminded him he had to answer it. It was Mabel Heartright. She was double-checking about the arrangements for the Thanksgiving potluck. "Is Beth Anne going to be in charge of the turkey this year?" she wanted to know. Inside Pastor Zackery wanted to scream, "Why don't you ask her?" Instead he calmly replied, "My wife, no doubt, will be very happy to take on the responsibility as she has done the past three years. However, I really shouldn't speak for her. It would be better if you contacted her yourself. She has a doctor's appointment today. Call her around four o'clock and she should be home." Mabel responded that she should have thought of that and that she would call her later. Putting down the phone after what seemed like the millionth interruption, Pastor Zackery thought of his wife.

Beth Anne Priest. She was still pretty. Her fifty-five years were well concealed and not by makeup. She just still looked so young. A smile of pride crossed the pastor's face. Beth Anne had always supported his ministry. She was willing to take on any task that needed to be done. Often Pastor Zackery had said to her that without her his ministry would be so ineffective. He never revealed just how ineffective he really felt he was. "I'd have washed out of the ministry long ago without Beth," he admitted out loud.

The thoughts of his wife brought joy and pain. It was fun being around her. People always commented about her laugh and her smile. She was great at listening. Many of the women in the congregation, particularly the younger women, would come to her for counseling. Pastor Zackery was not threatened in the least. He valued her ministry, but he alone among his members, past or present, knew the depths of her anguish. Beth Anne was unable to have a child. She was infertile. That word sounded so clinical, so harsh. Up until her fortieth birthday each month was like a roller coaster ride. Following her time of the month she spent a week in the dumps. Then came a week of pulling herself out of the dumpster. Then a week of convincing herself that this time she might be lucky. Temperature checks. Plenty of rest. Vitamins. Expensive medicine. Once she even bought her husband boxer shorts. She was convinced by a magazine article that that might be the answer. It wasn't—that month or any month. Her emotions nose-dived toward the miry pit on a very regular basis. Each visit to the maternity ward, each baby shower, each baptism reopened the wound. Since forty or so, Zackery couldn't remember exactly when, Beth Anne had reconciled herself to the fact that she would never have children. It was a bitter pill to swallow. Some days were better than others. For the most part she coped with the pain, but it was chronic. It would be always present.

Pastor Zackery sat at his desk. As he did every October he read through the Christmas story several times. This year he couldn't focus. He was bone-tired physically and spiritually he was parched as Indian corn. Zackery went into the dimly lit sanctuary to pray. He kneeled at the altar rail. The prayer grew out of his great frustration with the ministry, his wife's pain that only he knew, and the memories of Christmas sermons in the past when he had spoken assuredly about the hope, joy, peace and glory of Christmas. This year it all seemed so trite. How could he do justice to the Advent Season when everything he preached would be such a stark contrast to his own life? Tears welled up in the corners of his eyes. Before he could grab a Kleenex from the ready supply at the prayer rail, several salty tears pocked the surface of the page of the open Bible in front of him.

As if someone turned the dimmer switch to full brightness, the sanctuary was resplendent with light. It took several moments for his eyes to adjust; when he could see again, he wasn't quite sure he believed what he saw. There, standing in his chancel, was an angel. No wings. No halo. No silver tinsel. But he was sure it was an angel, even before the angel spoke. The words confirmed his belief. "Don't be afraid, Zackery." He hadn't thought he was afraid, but for a split second he diverted his gaze from the heavenly being to his hands. He realized he was shaking uncontrollably. The angel continued speaking. "Your prayer has been heard, Zackery. Your wife Beth Anne will have a son. You will name him John. You will be filled with unspeakable joy and gladness, and many other people will rejoice at his birth."

This message did not compute. He thought silently, "I haven't prayed for a child in many years. I have prayed that God would comfort Beth Anne. That God would somehow make up for her great loss. But a son? I haven't prayed that way since she passed through menopause." Then he blurted out, "How can this be? I'm getting old and my wife is ... well, it is not physically possible for her to have a child. Don't you know, she is fifty-five years old!"

The angel replied. "I am Gabriel. I stand in the presence of God and I have been sent to speak to you this good news. But now, because you did not believe my words, which will be fulfilled in their time, you will be mute, unable to speak, until the day these things occur."

With that the angel departed. He didn't leave in a huff. No, before leaving he again put his hand on the stunned pastor and whispered the words, "Don't be afraid. Everything will happen as I have said." Zackery didn't really see the departure. The angel was there speaking words of comfort, and then he was gone. Zackery touched his shoulder where the angel's hand had been.

The phone began to ring again. This time it was kind of an insistent ringing. Normally he would have let it ring. But this time he got up and went to answer it. Just doing something normal would help clear the fog from his mind. He needed clarity. He needed to be able to know reality from vision, fact from dream.

In the outer office he picked up the phone. Instantly he recognized the voice. It was Beth Anne. Something was wrong. No, different. His mind was still misted over. "Zack!" Beth Anne almost shouted. "I've got good news!" She rushed on, not giving him a chance to speak. "I'm calling from Doctor Williams' office. Honey, you're not going to believe this. I'm pregnant! We're going to have a baby! Can you believe it? Zack, honey? Are you there? Say something. Speak to me, honey."

The phone line was silent. It wasn't because Zack did not want to speak. He simply was unable to do so.

Cairo, Egypt
December 1994

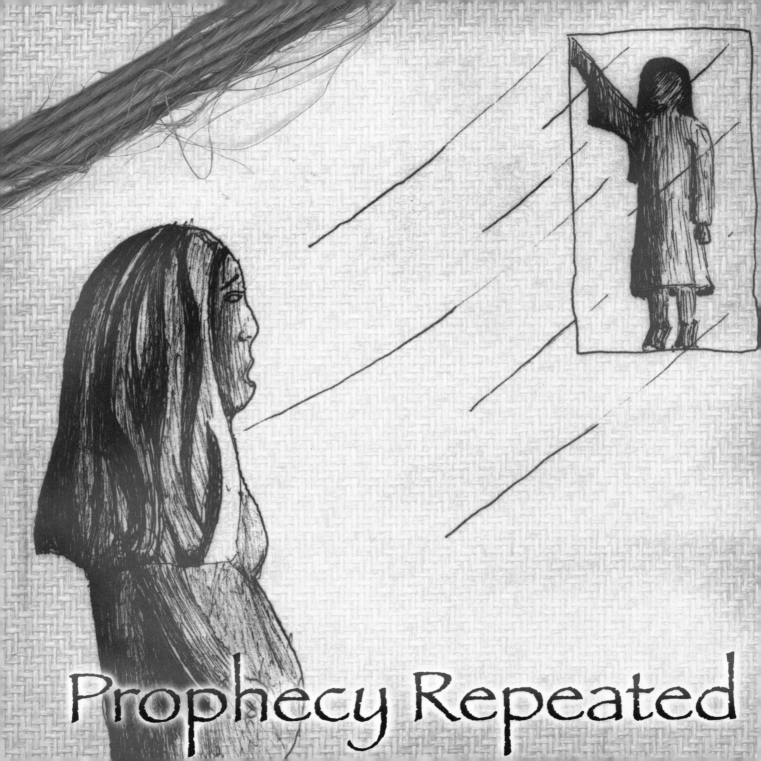

ven the smell of food made her sick. As she curled up on her pallet, the events of the month paraded through her mind. An angel's visit, a staggering message, pregnancy without ever having been touched by a man, so many explanations, an uncomfortable and hurried trip to avoid scorn, and a joyous and mysterious meeting with her cousin, Elizabeth.

Mary paused to gain strength from her meeting with Elizabeth—to remember. Elizabeth had called her blessed. "She said I was blessed 'because I believed that the Lord would keep his promise.' " Another wave of nausea rampaged through her tired frame. Elizabeth entered the darkened room with a cool cloth to wipe her dampened brow. Mary trembled. It was fear of the unknown more than a chill. Nonetheless, Elizabeth pulled the woolen blanket up over the teenager's shoulders.

"What did I say yesterday?" she asked timidly. Elizabeth knew exactly what she was speaking about. The words had been so beautiful, so prophet-like. Elizabeth had put them to memory. She instinctively knew these were words that spilled forth from a heart that had been in the presence of God.

Elizabeth leaned close to the younger woman and began to recite the most beautiful words outside of the Psalter that she had ever heard. Elizabeth spoke the words with feeling. A flame of unspeakable hope blazed in her eyes. The power of the words and the glow of hope soothed the trembling Mary.

> My heart sings within me.
> I cannot refrain from praising God.
> Praise the Lord!

I rejoice that God has finally come as Savior.
God cares for me.
Therefore, I give up all rights to myself.
I am God's servant.
He can do anything he wants to with me.

When people see me,
they will no longer shake their heads in scorn
or point accusing fingers at me.
No, they will say that God has blessed me.

Mary put her hand on Elizabeth's arm. "Did I really say that?" Her soul longed for Elizabeth's affirmative response. When it came she sighed deeply as if relieved to hear such good news.

Elizabeth continued her recitation.

God has done marvelous things for me.
God is holy.
But his holiness never overshadows his mercy.
God is ready to shine his glorious mercy on
anyone who worships him.

The Lord has lifted his powerful arm and
the proud have fled away.
God has begun a great exchange:
Powerful rulers have been replaced by the humble.
Yes, the humble now reign in the very seats of power.

"Can it be?" Mary interrupted. "Will God use the small child in my womb to do such marvelous things?"

Placing her hand gently on Mary's forehead Elizabeth said, "Listen, my child. You said more. You prophesied even greater things.

> The hungry will have their fill,
> but those who are rich will go away empty-handed.
> God will enter in on the side of his people Israel.
> He will show them the blessings of his mercy.
>
> God is now ready,
> and has in fact begun to fulfill his promises to his people.
> What he began with Abraham
> and spoke about in the prophets of old
> he is now ready to accomplish."

Mary smiled weakly and then drifted off to sleep. It was the first good sleep she had had since the angel first appeared to her. It was a sleep of quiet assurance. The leaning fence post of her faith had been shored up. Her own words of prophecy had straightened and strengthened her commitment to follow God's plan for her life, no matter what the cost.

When Mary woke her morning sickness was gone, and it never returned. In the same way that the morning sickness had faded and been replaced by the glow of motherhood, so, too, had her doubt and fear been superceded by her confidence in God's care and purposes.

Yet, that God had seen fit to choose her was a continuous marvel to Mary.

Cairo, Egypt
November 1994

Taxes: An Instrument in God's Hands?

Luke 2:1–7

 ho would have ever thought that anything good would come out of an across-the-board tax increase? The present tax system was already squeezing the breath out of the people. Now it appeared the Romans wanted to drain the blood out of their subjects as well.

It was bad enough when the taxes went to improve their roads, their water supply, and their fortifications. At least Herod, greatly disliked for his heavy taxes, had rebuilt the temple. But this new tax was something else altogether. The people could feel it in their bones. This new tax would go to support a hated, occupying military force. It would provide an extravagant life for a limited few in a decadent capitol city far away from Palestine. It might even be used to worship and glorify a man who claimed to be God. Military might and extravagant lifestyles were one thing. Being taxed to support blasphemy of the most revolting kind was something the Jewish people simply couldn't stomach.

God was well aware of the matter of unjust taxation. He recognized the hardship that it placed on peoples everywhere. He was grieved by the suffering that came with heavy-handed taxation. The improper expenditure of the money stripped from the poor made him angry. Yet, God saw the bigger picture. God knew that this soul-sapping taxation was the perfect way to fulfill what he had said long ago through one of his prophets. In a miraculous way, God was about to demonstrate his sovereignty. God was in the process of weaving a mandatory census and the resulting increased taxes into his tapestry of redemption. God's design combined the good and the not so good, the pure and the tainted, the amazing and the ordinary. Imagine, God even used a world class leader with divine aspirations and a humble carpenter whose only aspirations were focused on the mere survival of his family.

Joseph accepted the news of the new tax stoically. That he was being forced to pay anything to Rome at all bothered him, yet he was not a radical. He was no revolutionary advocating the overthrow of the enemy. He didn't even demonstrate for the repeal of the new tax law.

Joseph knew that this year he would have a much higher tax assessment. He had recently married and his wife was expecting. Three heads, all carrying a price that had to be paid. Joseph laughed sarcastically to himself. "Who will buy my head back when I can no longer pay these outrageous taxes?" He knew very well that there was no one to buy him back if he went under. He redoubled his efforts at his shop.

Not only did Joseph have to pay the taxes, but he had to get himself and his family to Bethlehem. That meant lost revenues from work, lost time. "At least we have family in Bethlehem; surely we can find a guest room with one of our kinfolk," he thought. A glimmer of hope sparkled momentarily in his eyes. "Maybe Mary will be able to have a little privacy." But a trio of villains—fatigue, worry, and hunger—chased the sparkle away. Joseph wondered about the child that was to be born within the month.

After a long, exhausting journey, Joseph and Mary arrived in Bethlehem.

They were both startled by what they saw. Just to enter the city they had to stand in a long queue. Hours passed. Mary grew more and more uncomfortable. The trip had been bad enough. She had been able to keep going because she knew that when she arrived in Bethlehem she would be able to lie down and get warm. Now at Bethlehem's gate, the prospect of a warm bed was like a mirage. From a distance it looked as if she could just reach out and touch it. Now that she had arrived at the spot of promised warmth and comfort, it had vanished. Mary's spirits fell. As she sat on the donkey's back Mary dreamed that she was holding a rope. "Just hang on to the rope," she repeatedly told herself. Yet her back, arms, and fingers grew weak. She was slipping, plunging into a dark....

Joseph saw Mary's heavy form sliding off the donkey. He moved quickly to catch her. Mary found herself in her husband's arms. He whispered into her ear. "It won't be long now, my little one." He used the expression of endearment he had started calling her long ago when she was still a child. It made her laugh. She was far from a "little one" now.

When they cleared the queue and entered the city, the mass of humanity was overpowering. People were everywhere. Joseph nimbly steered the donkey toward the home of his uncle. "He has a lovely guest room on top of his house," Joseph said confidently to his tired wife. The guest room was already full, two families occupied it. Nevertheless, Joseph's aunt invited them in, donkey and all.

The donkey was left with all the other animals down on the level of the doorway. You see, the main floor of the house doubled as a barn. The animals were down and the family lived up on a raised platform about head-high for the animals. At the edge of the living space were several feed boxes.

The next day all the men went out to stand in the long queues again to have the members of their family recorded and then to try to get some idea about what their new taxes would be. Joseph went reluctantly with the men folk from his family. The women assured him that they would take good care of Mary.

While Joseph stood in one unmoving line after another to try to pay his taxes, Mary gave birth to a son in a common one-room house-combination-barn. Joseph's aunt wrapped the baby up in some white clothes and laid him in a manger that had been filled with clean straw.

Not one person in Joseph's family knew that this child was the Messiah. Joseph and Mary remembered the angel's visits. They knew that this was a special child indeed. But no one told them, no one explained, that it was God's plan that they travel from Nazareth to Bethlehem. Even in their wildest dreams they could not have imagined that God would use this new series of taxes to fulfill his word. But it was true, nonetheless.

> But you, O Bethlehem of Ephrathah,
> who are one of the little clans of Judah,
> from you shall come forth for me
> one who is to rule in Israel,
> whose origin is from of old,
> from ancient days.

Cairo, Egypt
November 1994

The Garbage
Collector's Gift

The donkey cart was piled high with garbage that had been collected from around Cairo. The tandem of donkeys was barely able to pull the slow-moving garbage heap. Somewhere in their travels that day the two young barefooted boys had found a large box that read "Federal Express." That box had been positioned at the back of the cart. The sight of the international delivery service on the back of the donkey cart was a humorous thing to those who grasped the juxtaposition. The boys intended no joke or social commentary. They were merely trying to do their job efficiently. Other pieces of cardboard rimmed the top of their cart. All of this cardboard added extra height to the walls of the cart. Their strategy was obvious. With this extra cardboard the cart could hold much more garbage. Whether the bruised and battered donkeys could pull the extra weight was another matter. But the cart's new configuration had a serious flaw; that the well-used cardboard was simply not strong enough to corral the overflow. It was like trying to contain a mound of wet garbage in a rumpled cardboard box. With each jostle of the rutted road the cart would sigh and shudder and then spew forth some of the refuse that had been collected on the day's circuit.

The sun was setting across the Nile. The orangish light of dusk combined with the continuous smoke of the dump's rubbish heaps and the powder-like dust that filled the air made the area below the Moquattam Cliffs a ghostly place of shadows. In truth, it was a place of despair.

Even though the day was ending, the work was not. These two boys, and the six other members of their family, sorted the garbage together in silence. They were too tired to talk. Plastics in one pile. Metals in another. Food scraps to feed the pigs in yet another. Anything that was valuable for resale was gathered and given to the father. In the past weeks they found a silver spoon, a broken clock, and an electric toaster that was missing only the plug. Yesterday, the two boys had uncovered a deflated leather soccer ball. What a treasure! With their father's permission they were allowed to keep the ball. The find nourished the young boys' dreams about some day playing in the World Cup. "With a real ball, well, who can stop us now?" They had dreamed aloud together as they bounced along in the cart that very day.

Only when the days "catch" had been sorted did the family pause to eat. The fare was meager: cold potatoes, moldy bread, and smelly white cheese. They headed for their clapboard shanty. The soccer ball was their only entertainment but it was just too dark to play now. Besides, fatigue was settling in on all of them like a cold, damp fog. Their fatigue was mingled with a deadening hopelessness.

Suddenly an angel of the Lord appeared to them in glorious brightness.

Fear washed over the family. Instinctively they moved toward the father. It was protection they craved. They used their father's body as a human shield against the penetrating glory of the intruder.

"Don't be afraid," the angel said. "I have wonderful news for you and for everyone. Everyone is going to be joyful."

"*Joy*? I've forgotten what the word means." The thought rushed through the father's troubled mind.

"This very day," the angel continued, "in Shoubra El-Kheima a Savior has been born to you. He is God himself!"

The words were hard, astounding words. How could they understand such an announcement? What were they to do with such news?

And Shoubra El-Kheima? Wasn't that an industrial area? God coming to live in slums in the shadow of some dirty factory? The angel seemed to comprehend their fear, doubt, and misunderstanding. The instructions were not as hurried as the previous announcement. "You will know who the child is...."

"We are to see this One, this Child who is God himself? We will know him?" the words tumbled out of the father's mouth.

"Oh yes!" assured the angel. "You will find the baby wrapped in strips of cloth and lying in a feed box."

The mother broke in. "That is a sign? That is exactly what I did with each of my six children. How can that be a sign? Why every mother here in the dump has done the very same thing with their children."

The angel became a teacher. "You are so right, mother of Ishak," calling her by the name of her eldest son. "You have discovered the most important thing about this child. He has come to earth and he is just like you, except he is God."

Confusion spread across the faces of the men in her family, but the mother understood and took charge. "Come family," she ordered. "We will go search out this child. Quickly now, wash and make yourselves presentable."

As the family, clean as could be expected, tramped through the dust of Garbage City, the mother spoke up. "Father of Ishak, I wish we had some gift to give this Holy Child." The tone of her voice spoke volumes. She knew that they had nothing, yet, she needed to hear from her husband that they were doing their very best.

"My dear wife, you know we have nothing to give. The cost of our transportation to Shoubra El-Kheima alone will take all the money that we have. Our visit and our worship—these will be our gifts."

A look passed between the two youngest boys. The elder nodded to the younger. With great excitement the younger broke from the family procession and headed back toward their humble lodging.

Panting slightly, but smiling broadly nonetheless, the boy returned with the soccer ball under his arm. "Mama, if this boy who is God is just like us, we want to give him our ball." The brother just up in age from him nodded his approval.

"What about the World Cup?" his father asked with a proud look in his eyes. "We've played all along with our old cloth-stuffed ball. We'll just continue to do so. This boy that the angel told us about deserves the best that we have to give. He's the Lord!"

When the family returned from seeing the Savior, they were praising God and saying wonderful things about him. Everything had been just as the angel had told them. Their gift had been received and deemed worthy. Joy flooded their hearts and they shared the news about this child with everyone they met. All of Cairo listened and was very surprised.

Cairo, Egypt
November 1994

X-MAS DECORATIONS

The Empty Manger

The nativity set was a priceless family treasure. It was an heirloom. This nativity had been carved by Larry Konvick's father. His father had come to the United States as a boy from Eastern Europe shortly before the outbreak of the Great War. Each piece of this one-of-a-kind set had been intricately carved. The set had all the standard characters: Mary and Joseph, wisemen, shepherds, a wide variety of farm animals, and, of course, the Christ child. There was a hand-carved grotto and an attachable wooden star. Also included in this set were some extra items: a feed trough complete with real hay, a small wooden jewelry box, and two dainty cut glass bottles, complete with stoppers. The facial expressions on the wooden characters were amazing: a mixture of tiredness and joy on Mary's face; humility and honor on Joseph's; reverence, awe, and worship radiated from the faces of the wisemen; surprise and celebration shined in the faces of the shepherds.

Mary and Joseph were dressed as refugees from Eastern Europe. The wisemen were crafted to represent a Jewish rabbi, a Russian Cossack, and an Armenian priest. The shepherds were Gypsies. The Christ child appeared to be bundled in blankets. Most of his face was covered. His pug little nose and twinkling eyes could be seen in spite of the wrappings.

The Konvick family had a special tradition. During Advent they would set up the nativity in a prominent place in their home. Each piece was carefully unwrapped and positioned—each piece that is except the Christ child. The Christ child was always placed in the feed trough on Christmas Eve. On that night the family would gather round and read the Christmas story. Then one among them would have the honor of placing the blanketed-child in his place. This is the way Larry's father had done it, and Larry continued in this manner. It was such an ingrained practice that Helen Marie, the eldest daughter, was already planning to continue the tradition when the set was passed on to her.

The dinner dishes were finished and put away. Christmas carols were ringing throughout the house. The cider was steaming in the special Christmas mugs, pieces of cinnamon sticks floating on the top. The family gathered in the great room. A fire crackled in the fireplace. The room was lit only by the numerous candles that were all about. Everything was ready for the Konvick's family tradition to be recreated. This year Mother would read the Christmas story, using the massive family Bible.

While everyone got comfortable Larry asked in passing, "Elaine, where did we put the Christ child? I can't seem to find it in the box." The girls in the family rolled their eyes and each other. It was kind of a family joke. "The men in this family can never seem to find anything, Mom," Helen said to her mother. "I think it must be a gender thing." Everyone, including Larry, had a good laugh. But before long no one was laughing. No one could locate the Christ child. They searched and searched. Finally it was time to head out to the Christmas Eve Candles, Carols, and Communion service at church. Still no Christ child. As everyone put on boots, coats, scarves, and gloves, Elaine said, "We just can't have a Christmas without the Christ child. When we get back from church we must find him." There was a note of urgency in her voice. At church that evening the pastor retold the Christmas story. Pastor Frank was such a good storyteller, it wasn't long before each person in attendance was listening in focused concentration.

"… and as the shepherds went up toward Bethlehem they discussed among themselves what the announcement could mean. The trusting one among them recited the words that the angel had said, 'You will find the baby wrapped in swaddling cloths and lying in a manger.' The child among them was almost giddy with anticipation. The elders were more sober, yet filled with an inexpressible joy.

"As they came into the main court of the town they noticed that it was jammed with people. 'How among all these people are we going to find the child we have been told about?' said the more skeptical shepherd. 'The angel said that we will find him, and we will find him,' said the determined one. 'Find him or not, I believe,' said the trusting one. 'Let's quit talking and just find him,' said the eager one. The child said, 'Oh, I just want to see him. Do you think I can hold him?'

"On the outskirts of the town the five shepherds found a humble dwelling that was bathed in unmistakable light. 'We have found the place,' said the trusting one. 'I knew we would find the place,' echoed the determined one. 'Hang on, we haven't actually seen the child,' said the skeptical one. 'Let's knock on the door and see if this is the right place,' said the eager one. The child was already at the door knocking.

"All five were invited in. They saw Mary and Joseph…." Then the pastor gave a long pause. "… but they found no child wrapped in swaddling clothes." The pastor made a movement as if he were going to sit down, as though he had finished his meditation. A child in the startled congregation shouted out in frustration, "Where did they put the baby? We can't have a Christmas story without the baby!"

It was exactly the reaction the pastor was hoping to generate with his story. He turned back to face the congregation. He was smiling. "My friends, of course they found the baby, just as the angel had said they would. Each one of the five shepherds was strengthened in the faith. Each one was filled with joy. Each one was bursting at the seams to tell everyone they met about the angel's message, about God's visitation, and about their personal experience with the child and his family."

The pastor went on with his application. "Earlier in December I attended a winter music program at my daughter's school. When I was young these were called Christmas programs and, of course, we sang some seasonal favorites like 'Deck the Halls' and 'Jingle Bells'; we also unashamedly sang 'Away in a Manger,' 'Joy to the World,' and 'Silent Night.'

"Our country is trying desperately to have Christmas with Santas, gifts, tinsel, and family get-togethers, but without Christ. This must never be. We who are believers must never allow the world around us to determine the meaning of Christmas or set limits on our expression of joy, wonder, and thanksgiving at Christmas. Christ did not come to establish a holiday and then go away and be forgotten. NO! He came to save his people from their sins." With that, the pastor led the people in a most meaningful celebration of Communion.

When the Konvicks returned home, each one was struck by the timeliness of the pastor's message. In the past few years they had faithfully observed their tradition, carefully set out the nativity, read the story, and finally laid the child to rest in the manger. Everything was according to plan. But in their hearts had they really been leaving Christ out of their celebration? The father asked each family member to think about that question and to repent, if necessary.

On Christmas morning the carved Christ child had still not been found. The empty manger in the nativity became a conscious reminder that they would never intentionally allow Christ to be excluded from Christmas.

As the Konvick family began to distribute their gifts, they found, buried at the back of the tree under a colorfully wrapped package, the wooden infant. When the child was found the whole family celebrated with unbounded joy. All the gifts were forgotten. The big family Bible was again brought out. The story was read. And Larry gently placed the child in the manger.

The family tradition had been upheld. The nativity set was again complete. Christ was again at the center of every aspect of the Christmas celebration in the Konvick house.

Cairo, Egypt
December 1994

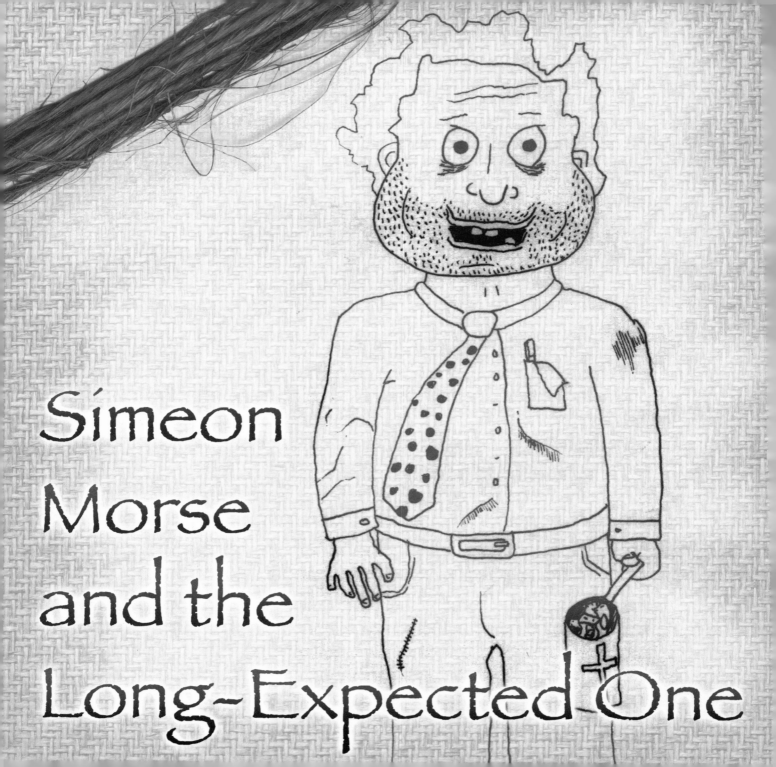

Simeon
Morse
and the
Long-Expected One

 imeon Morse had been around the church a long time. He was a squarish sort of man, very unkempt. Frankly, he smelled. The last pastor, Reverend Cook, had worked a deal with Simeon. If Simeon would take a bath each and every Saturday night, then Simeon could help collect the offering. If not, Simeon could not take part. The pastor also took Simeon down to the Goodwill Store and bought Simeon a second suit and several changes of clothes. Each Sunday morning Simeon was to drop his soiled clothes off at the church office. Pastor Cook would make sure that the clothes were laundered during the following week. This was also the time the pastor would decide if Simeon was presentable to work as an usher on that particular Sunday. It was a good plan and it worked, more or less, during the tenure of Reverend Cook.

After seven years, however, Reverend Cook moved on to another church. During the interim, even important things fell through the cracks. The weekly checkup for Simeon fell by the way-side. With no one to monitor his condition, Simon's condition worsened. He reverted back to his old habits. He wore his favorite suit and favorite shirt day and night. The blue serge suit was always wrinkled. It appeared that he slept in it; in fact, he did. His white shirt was any-thing but. Coffee stains were visible on the right side and blue ink on the left. It was as if a fountain pen had exploded in his pocket. His body odor was unbearable. People began to complain to the Elders' Board. What could be done about Simeon Morse? When John Jacobs arrived on the scene Simeon Morse was an inherited problem. The Elders were more than happy to turn Simeon's situation over to "Pastor John," as he preferred to be called.

What Pastor John discovered was that everyone agreed that Simeon was a fine old man. He might not be that bright, but no one ever questioned his faithfulness to the church. If the doors were open, Simeon was there. If chairs needed to be set out, Simeon was ready. If hymnals were needed, Simeon was a willing volunteer. If bulletins or communion cups needed to be collected from the pews after the service, Simeon was your man. Everyone also agreed that Simeon loved children. He always had a double pack of gum ready to hand out to the children following the service. Children seemed to gravitate to Simeon. The younger they were, the less they noticed his body odor.

Pastor John again instituted the former pastor's "must wash, must change" policy. Simeon seemed comfortable with it. He conformed, most of the time. Pastor John looked for ways to include Simeon in ministry. Finally, Simeon was charged with and given sole leadership of "Simeon's Helping Hand Task Force." Simeon was a committee of one. His task was to help the pastor when he dedicated infants. Pastor John would call on Simeon to escort the families forward. Simeon would hand out the roses to the mothers and certificates to the fathers. Often, if the infant's siblings grew restless during the pastor's dedication prayer, Simeon would silently pacify the children. He was amazing at doing this. He could calm a squirming child in moments. Pastor John was pleased. The Elders were nothing short of speechless. And Simeon—he was in heaven when he could perform his ministry within the body.

A wonderful transformation was taking place in Simeon's life. The more responsibility he was given the more he responded. Bathing became a normal Saturday night activity. Now it was true that one bath a week could not remove all of the smell that accumulated over the course of a week, but his fragrance was such a change for the better that no one complained.

On one particular Sunday morning a poor migrant family, Jose and Maria Garcia and their infant son, Jésus, came to church. They were in the area to pick tomatoes. They spoke Spanish and only a smattering of English. How they found the church, no one knows.

Simeon always made it a point to sit on a beige metal folding chair by the entrance to the church. If newcomers would arrive late he was always there to greet them with a friendly smile and handshake. The Simeon Morse Task Force saw a need and filled it.

When the Garcias walked through the door, of course, Simeon was right there. In his sensitive way, Simeon quickly realized that there was something special about this family. Although Simeon couldn't speak a word of Spanish, he and this young migrant family began to converse.

The pastor saw all of this taking place at the back of the church. He wondered what was happening. A sort of nervous tingling passed down his spine. Pastor Jacobs knew something remarkable was about to happen—in fact, was happening—but he couldn't figure it out. "Who are those people talking with Simeon?" he thought to himself. "What do they want? Do they need food from the food pantry? Are they passing through and need a place to stay?" His mind crackled with this kind of static like an old Philco radio. All the while he sang three verses of "Holy, Holy, Holy."

At the end of the hymn the pastor was to stand and lead the congregation in a time of corporate prayer. Pastor Jacobs was preempted. Up the center aisle marched Simeon and the Garcia family. Simeon, not surprisingly, was carrying the infant. Simeon began to praise God in a voice loud enough to be heard by all but gentle enough not to startle the baby.

> Lord, I am your servant,
> and now I can die in peace,
> because you have kept
> your promise to me.
>
> With my own eyes I have seen
> what you have done
> to save your people,
> and the foreign nations
> will also see this.
>
> Your mighty power is a light
> for all nations,
> and it will bring honor
> to your people Israel.

The congregation sat in their places without moving. They were stunned. Pastor Jacobs stood at the microphone and tried to think of something to say. He was completely at a loss, yet within, his heart was praising God with jubilant songs. José and Maria stood before the gathered community a bit perplexed. They had understood every word that Simeon had said. It was as if he had spoken in Spanish to them and simultaneously in English so the people could understand.

The silence in the sanctuary that morning was electrifying. Simeon turned to bless José and Maria. "May God bless you and keep you. May God give you wisdom as you raise this child. May you always be sensitive to the purposes of God. God has a special purpose for this child. In his mysterious way he has chosen you to bring baby Jésus up to maturity. Never forget that we in the community of faith are charged this morning to help you in your task. We are committed to stand with you in order that baby Jésus will know God and in time tell others about God." All this time Simeon had either been looking at the baby or at the couple. As Simeon finished his words of charge and blessing to the couple, he lifted his eyes to the congregation. As if on cue, the gathered community said reverently, "Amen."

Then Simeon handed the infant back to his mother. He spoke again. "This child of yours will cause many people to fall and others to stand. The child will be a warning sign. Many people will reject him, and you, Maria, will suffer as though you had been stabbed by a hunting knife. But all this will show what people are really thinking."

Maria visibly shuddered. The words had a haunting quality about them. Simeon led the young family toward the front pew. It was always vacant, and today was no exception.

Pastor Jacobs' tongue was loosed and he led the congregation in a service of praise. The funny thing was that, even though it was July, the hymns that flooded the pastor's heart were Christmas carols. Once it began, the service took on a life of its own. One after another people requested the familiar carols, often sung but seldom meditated upon. Today the words to each carol rang with truth. It was as though through this young migrant family and faithful Simeon, the story of Christmas had been recreated in their midst. And it had.

The final carol before the benediction was "Come, Thou Long-Expected Jesus."

> Come, Thou long-expected Jesus,
> Born to set Thy people free;
> From our fears and sins release us;
> Let us find our rest in Thee.
> Israel's Strength and Consolation,
> Hope of all the earth Thou art;
> Dear Desire of every nation,
> Joy of every longing heart.
>
> Born Thy people to deliver,
> Born a child and yet a King;
> Born to reign in us forever,
> Now Thy gracious Kingdom bring.
> By Thine own eternal Spirit
> Rule in all our hearts alone;
> By Thine all sufficient merit
> Raise us to Thy glorious throne.

Cairo, Egypt
November 1994

The Signature
of Her Life

 She was a stooped-shouldered, haggard-looking woman. Like an ancient tapestry she was well-worn, frayed around the edges, colors faded. Yet, in the same way that a handmade silk carpet increases in value over time, so, too, had this woman's value to the community of faith multiplied.

Her walk was slow, a too-tired-to-pick-up-her-feet kind of walk. When she moved through the temple area everyone knew that Anna was coming. Her slippers never left the floor as she shuffled and slid along. The sound was distinctive. It was part of her signature.

Anna's black *galebeyah* formed another part of her unique signature. She had worn black mourning garb for some sixty-four years. Never did she wear anything else. If anyone deserved to be down on life, it was this woman. She had been married at a young age, barely a teen-ager. Her marriage was arranged for her, and her husband was a harsh man twice her age. Anna never experienced the joy of bearing children. She was barren. She became a widow after only seven years of marriage. She was just shy of twenty when she was joined by family and friends to bury her husband.

She was thin, exceedingly so. Her limbs were mere sticks. Her cheeks sunken. Her hands gnarled. Her skin almost translucent. All of these physical attributes were due, in no small part, to her age. Yet her condition was worsened by her constant state of fasting. Fasting was not a once or twice-a-year religious practice for Anna. It was the norm. Nonetheless, this frail-looking woman was surprisingly wiry, strong, and resilient, both in body and spirit. If ever there was a saint, it was Anna. Her spirituality was a marvel to behold and added an air of piety to her signature.

The amazing thing about Anna was not her outward appearance or her visible religious piety, although both were one of a kind. It was the captivating sparkle in her eyes. No one would have expected to see the childish delight that literally danced in her eyes as she went about her daily rituals in the temple courtyard. She radiated joy, the kind of joy that was contagious. She lent a spirit of expectation to her setting. Her inner joy added a special flair to her signature.

Day after day Anna ministered in the temple. She was counselor, confidante, and confessor. She really filled the priestly role in a remarkable way. By means of her life experiences and deep piety, she was recognized as a living treasure within the religious community. Priests, rabbis, and scribes came to her. So, too, did the ordinary people. Everyone sought out her wisdom and, in the process, were warmed by her quick wit. Her wisdom gave her signature a certain levelness, a divine evenness. Her humor brought forth laughter.

Anna's signature had an unmistakable passion about it. She was passionate about her God. The more time slipped by, the more people's longing for Messiah's coming tended to wither like grapes that are left unplucked on the vine. Such was not the case with Anna. The more time passed, the more eager she became. She knew within her soul that one day she would see God's anointed. This passion was the driving force of her life, her reason for existence. The signature of her life was bold and forthright as a result.

As Anna was on her way to the temple courtyard, she was greeted by several children—"her children," she called them. She lovingly tousled their heads as she called out greetings to their parents. Near the entrance to the temple court a voice called out her name. "Anna, can we talk?" The pain in the woman's words seemed to bounce like marbles down the cobblestone alley.

For almost an hour Anna listened as this woman poured out her soul. The woman's husband and only son had been arrested that very morning by the Romans. Her men folk were Zealots. Anna knew very well that the Romans dealt ruthlessly with Zealots. It was likely that this woman would not see her men folk for a long time, if at all. Anna cried with the woman. She prayed with her. She sat silently with her.

As Anna rose to leave, she promised her friend that she would return again the next morning. She would also speak to a leader of the Sadducees who was on fairly good terms with the Roman governor. Perhaps he could do something. Anna stood on the threshold of the house and embraced the woman one more time. In parting, the grieving woman asked Anna a question, "Will the Messiah really come or has God forgotten us?" Anna reached out with her bony finger and wiped a lingering tear from the woman's cheek. "Soon, my dear. Very soon." The passion of her words flowed from within. With that she shuffled away.

Anna almost missed the small family that day. They had come to the temple to give the customary sacrifice at the birth of their firstborn. The family was obviously poor, only able to afford a pair of pigeons. God spoke to Anna that morning as she watched the couple bundle up their child in preparation to leave the temple grounds. "This child is the Messiah." Her joy knew no bounds. God was going to fulfill his promises to Israel in the life of a little child. "How like our marvelous God," she whispered to herself.

She started to move toward the threesome but quickly recognized that too many people were in her way. She would never be able to navigate through the maze of people to be able to hold the child. She simply moved to one side and watched. Then she saw her dear friend Simeon. He too was waiting eagerly for the Messiah. As she leaned against the wall of the courtyard, she saw Simeon go up to the family and carefully take the child. Anna saw the explosion of joy on Simeon's face. She saw him speak with animation. She saw Simeon as he cradled the child in his arms and prayed a prayer of blessing on the child and his parents. This scene was a visible confirmation of God's whispered message.

Anna turned toward the stone archway that led from the temple grounds. She shuffled along the stone pavement. Before she told anyone else—and she would soon tell everyone she met—she must share this good news with her friend, the woman whose men folk had been arrested.

Cairo, Egypt
November 1994

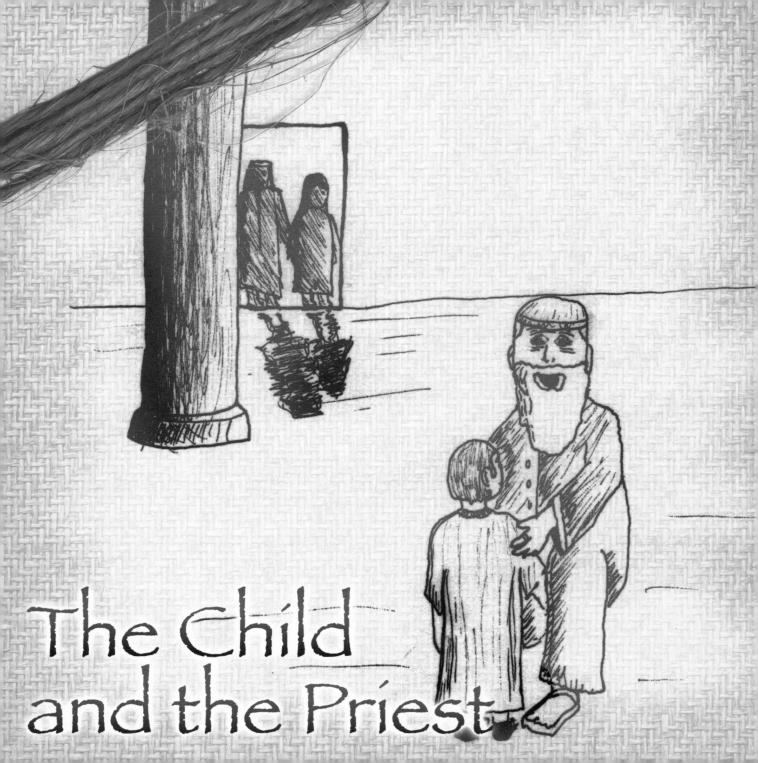

Luke 2:41–52; Isaiah 9:6–7

The child sat among the seminary professors and taught them. He didn't lecture or draw diagrams, yet his questions and insights penetrated to the heart of what was being discussed. His answers? Well—they were as if the Author of Life, using a twelve-year old vocabulary, was explaining how he had formed his creation and was now in the process of bringing redemption and deliverance to light. In this child, stuffy, visibly pious, religious practice and holy-sounding, textbookish, theological talk were shattered as surely as an eggshell gives way when it is crashed upon the lip of a skillet. His observations were fresh. His insight into the Scriptures sparkled with life.

At first bemused, then awestruck, these leaders and teachers of orthodoxy sat on the very edge of their cushions trying to drink in the full meaning of what this young lad was saying. Did any of these scholars who had studied and memorized vast tracts of Scripture think back to the words of Isaiah?

> For a child has been born for us,
> a son given to us;
> authority rests upon his shoulders;
> and he is named
> Wonderful Counselor, Mighty God,
> Everlasting Father, Prince of Peace.
> His authority shall grow continually,
> and there shall be endless peace
> for the throne of David and his Kingdom.
> He will establish and uphold it
> with justice and righteousness
> from this time onward and forevermore.
> The zeal of the Lord of hosts will do this.

The young boy had sat just outside the circle of well-polished gentlemen and listened. Dressed in his very best clothes, he still looked like a mongrel at a pedigree dog show. There was nothing about him that exuded confidence or wisdom. Humility and a certain down-home charm, maybe. Appearance-wise he was out of his league. Several times some of the assistants in the temple area had tried to chase the lad off. The boy persistently returned to the edge of the conversation. Finally, the most senior priest motioned to them to leave the boy alone. He was allowed to stay. "Who knows," the leader thought to himself, "maybe this child will grow up to be a leader in his home synagogue."

"Where are you from, my son?" the priest asked. All eyes in the circle turned to the boy.

"I am from Nazareth," he answered very politely. "I have come with my family to sacrifice for the Passover." The elderly priest smiled and called the boy over to his side. "My son, you and your family are doing an important thing. You have come to remember what God did for his people long ago." The priest had a cushion brought over so the boy could have something to sit on. He continued. The boy sat enthralled as the priest went back to the Exodus, the seminal event for the people of God.

The boy listened for a long time as the priest spoke of the plagues, the pharaoh, the death angel, the crossing of the Red Sea.

"It seems to me," the lad interjected, "that the Passover is important because it reminds us of God's deliverance."

The priest grinned broadly and patted the lad on the head. Speaking to the others in the circle he said, "This young twelve-year old has a better grasp of theology than many of my students." The learned men in the circle laughed and nodded in agreement.

As if to test the young boy, the priest asked, "This deliverance that you spoke of, how was it earned?"

If the priest didn't know better he would have thought by the expression on the boy's face that he had offended him. "Oh, sir, that's just it," the child took on the air of a teacher. "This deliverance was a gift. The deliverance symbolized by the Passover is a free and gracious gift."

Over the next hours the child led the leaders on a study of the concept of grace, first from the Law, then the Prophets, and finally from the Psalms. Old scholarly eyes, eyes that were thirsty for truth but had found so little in years of study, locked on the child.

Pilgrims came and went all during the time that the child spoke. The bleating of sheep and the plaintive cries of the animals being sacrificed could be heard in the background. Chanting and blessing-giving added to the religious noise in the temple area. The air was saturated with incense and smoke all mingled with the smells of animals and hot bodies. Yet none of this distracted the teacher-child or his students.

Who knows how long the session would have continued. Only when a nervous-looking couple came in and found their child was the spell broken. "Where have you been? We've been looking for you. Why have you troubled us?" the words tumbled out of the mouth of an anxious father, Joseph.

"We've been so worried," Mary said.

"Why were you searching for me? Didn't you know that I must be in my father's house?" Jesus said in perfect innocence. The words simply passed right over the heads of his parents. They did not understand.

At the words "my father's house," the priest sat bolt upright. "Could this be the One?" he asked himself. "Is this the One who will lead us? Is he our deliverance?" He pushed the thought from his mind. "God certainly does remarkable things, and I am indeed thankful for this gifted child. God has given me some grist for thinking. But when the Messiah comes, well, he will be a smashing stone* that will wipe away our enemies. This child is gentle and ever so polite. He is far from a smashing stone."*

The priest stretched his weary back and watched the young family until they were out of sight. He sighed deeply. "Now back to my religious duties," he said to himself. His thoughts of the Messiah and his coming, of God's gracious deliverance and the teachings of this remarkable lad receded in his mind as he was swept away by the demands of the ritual sacrifices.

Cairo, Egypt
November 1994

*See Daniel 2:24–45

Stories Woven From Isaiah's Threads

And It Came To Pass

Isaiah 7:14; Luke 1:26–56; 2:1–20

Martha and Roger Campbell had been married sixty-two years. They had a big family. It was a Christmas tradition in the Campbell family to "gather the clan," as Grandpa Campbell put it. Now that I am grown up and part of an extended family of my own, I wonder how they managed. But they did. I have heard family members tell of being out sledding after opening their Christmas presents and having to be very careful negotiating the curve in front of Grandpa Campbell's place. Cars sporting license plates from the surrounding states were parked all along the street.

At Grandpa Campbell's place, before the family exchanged any gifts, they always read the Christmas story. Grandpa grew up reading the King James Version. To him it was *The* Holy Bible. He wasn't against other people using different translations, but for Martha and him, every other translation paled by comparison. And the Christmas story, well … one could not get the feeling of Christmas without the story being told in the *King's English*.

Jonathon Carter, the great-grandson of Grandpa Campbell, was five years old. He was the youngest child at the family Christmas gathering. According to the Campbell tradition, the youngest child always sat in the lap of the oldest adult present to hear the story read. Grandpa Campbell laughed as he said, "We may have to change that tradition if I stick around ten more years. Jonathon will be fifteen and I will be ninety-five." You can just picture the scene: old Grandpa Campbell seated in his Lazyboy rocker with Jonathan plopped on his lap. All the other extended family would be gathered around.

Grandpa Campbell began to read. He really didn't need the big family Bible, he had read this story so many times he knew the story frontward and backwards. Can you imagine the feeling he put into the story as he read? Long before I ever entered high school Grandpa Campbell had retired from teaching. He taught English literature and drama. He loved a good story; to Grandpa Campbell, no story ever written could compare with the story of the coming of the Christ child. It must have been glorious for the adults to hear him speak the words of the angel of the Lord. "Hail, thou art highly favored, the Lord is with thee: blessed art thou among women." Or, to hear him repeat Elizabeth's astounding greeting to Mary. "For, lo, as soon as the voice of thy salutation sounded in my ears, the babe leaped in my womb for joy." When Grandpa Campbell got to the part about Mary and Joseph reaching Bethlehem, he must have been in rare form indeed. "And so it was, that, while they were there, the days were accomplished that she should be delivered." As I said, it must have been great for the adults, but for the young ones it made little sense.

Several times in the story Grandpa Campbell repeated the words, "And it came to pass." It is true that Steven Carter and his cousin Mitch Campbell always got a kick out of that part because, as they always joked, "It was one of the times football is mentioned in the Bible." It was an old joke, taught to them by none other than Grandpa Campbell himself.

To hear the reading with all the "thee's" and "thou's" and "lo's" and "salutations," well, for five-year old Jonathon it was just too much to bear. Then on top of all that, to hear the phrase "it came to pass" repeat— this just didn't compute. After the third "and it came to pass," Jonathon put his finger up to his grandfather's lips to stop the story. It was like one of my children today hitting the pause button on the videotape player. The story stopped. A freeze-frame look appeared on Grandpa Campbell's face. All eyes shifted from Grandpa Campbell to Jonathon.

"Grandpa, you keep saying that it came to pass. What does 'it came to pass' mean?" A gentle laughter passed through the family. Some of those on the outside of the ring did not hear clearly. Those who had heard shared Jonathon's question. Grandpa waited for quiet.

"Some people think that those words were just an old way of telling the story, my son," he said as he tousled Jonathon's blond head. "But for me it has great meaning." A hush came over the room. "'It came to pass' means that God was doing exactly what he said he would do." "You mean by sending Jesus to us?" remarked Mitch. "Exactly, Mitch."

"Oh, I suppose you could read the story without 'and it came to pass' and catch the meaning just fine. But what would you be missing? You would be missing that special reminder that the elderly Elizabeth, teenage mother, carpenter father, and the shepherds to boot, were fulfilling God's holy plan.

The grandfather flipped back through his Bible to Isaiah and read these words.

"And, lo, a virgin shall conceive and bear a son, and shall name him Immanuel." He thumped his Bible as if to emphasize the point. "God said it!" he affirmed. And the family chorused back, "And it came to pass!"

Grandpa Campbell didn't live another ten years, but, according to tradition, two of Grandpa's last three years on earth, Jonathon Carter sat on his lap. The final Christmas Grandpa spent with us, I, Jonathon, was bumped out of the seat of honor by Stephanie, the newest great-grandchild.

And it came to pass, in February, following my unseating, that Grandpa Campbell died and went to his eternal home with the Christ he celebrated, worshiped, and loved.

Cairo, Egypt
December 1994

Out of the
Darkness Into Faith

 man felt so lonely. Her husband, Maged, was off in Europe some place. She didn't really know where he was. Her marriage had been a weak one from the start. Maged was more concerned about his business than he was about his family, or at least that was the impression he dropped here and there like discarded-dirty clothes about their spacious apartment. Money was not the problem. A lack of love—that was the problem.

It didn't help that tonight was Christmas Eve. Iman had taken her only son to the large Coptic Orthodox Church not far from her home in Heliopolis, a wealthy suburb in Cairo. The church was full to running over. Iman looked around. She didn't recognize anyone near her. Maybe most of these in attendance were once-a-year visitors like herself. Maybe they were regular attenders and she just didn't recognize them because her attendance was so sporadic. Iman began to feel conspicuous. Although no one was looking, she wanted to hide. She felt like she was wearing a sign that announced, "This lady does not belong here." "Funny," she thought to herself, "my name means *faith* and I can't even live up to it."

The priest chanted the liturgy and Iman had a hard time keeping up. Michael, her son, had fallen asleep during the mass. He rested heavily on her lap. The space between the pew was extremely narrow. Her knees were pinned against the bench in front. Even before the service had begun, she was uncomfortable. She wished she had held her ground at the end of the row. Latecomers had pushed her toward the center. She was boxed in as surely as if a lorry had double-parked beside her car. She was forced to stay for the entire service, and the Christmas Eve service that year was of record length.

At the end of the mass she tried to make a beeline for the exit. The only problem was that only one exit was open. Because of the large seasonal attendance, it took Iman almost fifteen minutes to clear the large wooden door at the rear of-the sanctuary. As she shuffled along trying to help her sleepy ten-year old keep his balance, she attempted to block out the roar of noise around her. It was happy noise full of Christmas greetings. Once or twice, when saw someone that she knew, she pasted on her "all occasion" smile. She hated that plastic face but right now it came in very handy. It covered her pain and loneliness. It was like a security light that lit up the area surrounding her but did nothing to penetrate the inky blackness of her soul.

She had parked a considerable distance from the church. The walk away from the celebrative atmosphere of the church was refreshing. But the streets were so dark. The farther she went from the church, the darker it became. Once she turned around and looked back. Light seemed to spill out of the church onto the steps in front. A chill passed down her spine. She felt an involuntary shiver.

Once in her car the drive home was uneventful. When she arrived at her apartment, it took no time to realize that there was no electricity. No electricity meant no lights and no lift. She trudged up the stairs to the seventh floor. At each landing she said a curse under her breath.

She groped her way to her front door. She located it but not before she knocked over the water jar that she had recently filled with an ivy that the florist had promised could grow in dark places. Now it didn't make any difference. The plant lay mingled with broken pottery pieces and dirt. "I'll clean the mess up tomorrow when I have some light to see what I'm doing," she promised herself.

Finding the right key for the door was no easy task, but finally she was inside. She found the candle and matches that she had stashed near the entrance for such occasions. The electricity in her neighborhood of Cairo was always erratic.

With great effort she got Michael to bed. He was such a sound sleeper. "Just like his father," Iman thought.

The apartment was cold. Iman bundled up in bed. Sleep eluded her. Thoughts of happy Christmases gone by flooded her mind—her father, recently dead of cancer, dressed as Father Christmas. Family meals. Laughter. Being together. Light.

Iman fell into a troubled sleep. She dreamed. She was walking down a crowded street in Heliopolis. People were happy. Joy was all around her. But she had no joy. Then all at once the streets were empty. It was inexplicable. Metal shutters on storefronts slammed shut. Children were rushed inside. The religious noise of the area was cut short. Iman was left standing all alone in Roxi Square. Not a bus. Not a taxi. Not a person. Darkness descended. It was oppressive. It felt demonic. She began to sob.

In his room, Michael was awakened by his mother's crying. That he even woke up was a miracle. He went to comfort his mother. As he entered her room he reached for the switch and flicked on the light. The darkness fled away. Sometime in the night the electricity had been restored.

Michael came to his mother and simply cradled her head in his arms. He didn't say anything until her sobbing ceased. Then he kissed her on the forehead and said, "I love you, Mommy." That was all he said. Iman hugged him tightly. "I love you, too, Misho," she said, using his pet name.

When Michael was tucked back in bed, Iman knew that she would not be able to sleep again that night. She went out to her living room looking for something to read. Nothing appealed to her. She was restless. "The Bible; why not read the Bible?" The thought came to her from outside herself. She hadn't read the Bible in years.

It took her several moments to find one. She had no idea where to read. She thought of the Christmas story. "Yes," she decided, "as soon as I get a comforter I'll read the Christmas story. It's cold in here," she was saying to herself as she started to stand. The Bible slipped off her lap and sprawled out in front of her. She quickly picked it up. She may not have been in church for a long time, and she may not have read the Bible recently, but she still had a healthy respect for it. Maybe it could be called a fear of the Bible. Whatever the feeling, Iman picked the holy book up carefully.

The words at the top of the page caught her attention.

> The people who walked in darkness
> Have seen a great light;
> Those who lived in a land of deep darkness—
> On them the light has shined.

She skimmed over the next few verses noting the words "joy," "rejoice," "exult," and "burdens broken." Her eyes focused again.

> For a child has been born for us,
> A son given to us;
> Authority rests upon his shoulders;
> And he is named
> Wonderful Counselor, Mighty God,
> Everlasting Father, Prince of Peace.

She instinctively knew these words spoke of Christ. She had heard them long ago in her mission school. But what struck her most was how in the midst of her darkness, a deep darkness of her soul, a child had come to her. He had turned on the lights. He had cradled her head. He had sat with her until her fear, loneliness, and depression had passed. He had tenderly said that he loved her.

In those moments, in the early morning hours of Christmas Day, Iman Bishara learned the significance of the day she had long celebrated. From that moment she began to live her life in accordance with her name.

Cairo, Egypt
December 1994

The Stump,
the Prophet,
and the People

The stump was weather-beaten, cracked and dry. No one really knew when the tree had been cut down. Even the elders in the community could not remember a time when the tree had borne its life-giving cones and given off that special aromatic freshness that this cedar was famous for. The tree had once thrived, so the community folklore said, but a disease had ravaged it from the inside out. It had been necessary to lop off the top section of the tree in hope that this would save the lower base. Such was not the case. In a matter of time the lower branches showed clear signs of the disease. The bark began to rot. The tree lost its green. The wood softened. The once-giant tree became the host for all sorts of insects and bugs. In the end it was determined that the tree was good only for the fire. And what a fire it was. Now all that was left was a knee-high, gnarled reminder of a tree, blackened with age.

The cedar stump sat in the center of the village. It was used for various purposes throughout the week. Mondays through Thursdays the stump was used as a hitching post for donkeys. On Saturdays and Sundays the stump became the center of the farmers' market. Often it served as a chopping block. Many a chicken lost its head on that stump. On Fridays the stump was transformed again. This time the stump took on a religious significance. It became the place where a small, seemingly insignificant community of the faithful would gather to remember. They would recite the stories of the past, the days gone by when people spoke of the possibility of living in relationship with God. They read from their holy history narratives of faithful kings and seers. They sang and chanted songs of victory. They prayed ritualized prayers in hope that the prayers would break through the gray, overbearing skies and fly unfettered to a God who somehow still cared for them, still listened to them.

One Sunday an ancient-looking prophet came to the community. His anger glowed red-hot as he witnessed a heavy set man in a bloody apron decapitate chicken after chicken on the stump. The following days were almost as bad. The prophet's heart was grieved beyond measure to see donkeys tethered to that very same stump.

On Friday the prophet took his place beside the stump early in the morning. He was there long before the group of believers assembled. He prayed and communed with God. The prophet was on his knees praying as the people gathered. They had witnessed the prophet in their community throughout the week and had wondered what the holy man wanted. A few had approached the prophet at odd times during the week but the man seemed to speak nonsense. As the word spread throughout the community, people began to give the seer a wide berth. Now, on this day of gathering, the faithful, or, as others in the community had begun to call them, "The Holy Stumpers," assembled. It was obvious that the prophet wanted to speak to them. They waited nervously, expectantly.

The old man spoke. "A shoot shall blossom from this stump," he began. As he spoke he fingered the deep grooves where year after year the butcher's cleaver had done its bloody job. "A branch shall grow out of these roots. God himself will cause this to happen."

The community of the faithful sat in rapt attention. They had longed for such a message, longed to hear words of hope and promise. It was almost too good to be true. What the prophet said next was most amazing. He removed his hand from the stump and stretched his hand out toward the crowd. "This cedar stump is only a symbol. You are the true stump." A look of confusion passed through the assembly. "I hear what the people in this town say about you. They call you 'The Holy Stumpers' and that is exactly what you are. You are the righteous remnant." Surprise registered on the people's faces. The prophet continued. His words were as poetic as they were prophetic.

> Out of you will come a leader for God's people.
> The spirit of the Lord shall rest on him,
> the spirit of wisdom and understanding,
> the spirit of counsel and might,
> the spirit of knowledge and the fear of the Lord.
>
> His delight shall be in the fear of the Lord.
> He shall not judge by what his eyes see,
> or decide by what his ears hear;
> but with righteousness he shall judge the poor,
> and decide with equity for the meek of the earth;
> he shall strike the earth with the rod of his mouth,
> and with the breath of his lips he shall kill the wicked.

Righteousness shall be the belt around his waist,
and faithfulness the belt around his loins.

The wolf shall live with the lamb,
the leopard shall lie down with the kid,
the calf and the lion and the fatling together,
and a little child shall lead them....

The earth will be full of the knowledge of the Lord
as the waters cover the sea.

"When, oh when, will all of this happen?" the people asked. The prophet never really said. What he did say was the flowering of the stump would be a sign that this righteous one was to be born. A passionate hope was planted within the breasts of the Stumpers.

The story of the prophet became the central story of the community of the faithful. Although the people in the vicinity didn't believe the words of the prophet, they allowed the religious among them to fence off the stump. The townspeople no longer tied their donkeys to the stump nor did they allow the butcher to continue his trade in that location.

Years passed. The story faded in importance for the people. They still called themselves "The Stumpers," although most didn't have the slightest idea where the name had come from or why they gathered about the worm-eaten stump. The prophet's words had become like the stump itself, lifeless. The prophet's words were repeated in rote fashion each time the community gathered. Yet they had no meaning.

One day a small child noticed a tiny sprig at the base of the stump. It was a finger of green pointing up at the sun. No one would listen to the child as he tried to make the people see. The sad truth was that even as this finger of life flowered and bloomed, the gathered community continued to recite the prophet's story but were blinded to the greening of the cedar. The child's words were a source of constant irritation to the Stumpers.

Cairo, Egypt
November 1994

A Christmas Miracle
in the Old City

I t was Christmas time in the city. The air was cold and damp. Snow flurries had been forecast. The skies were covered with leaden clouds, heavy with moisture driven by powerful winds. The gusts of wind seemed to threaten to rip open the low-lying clouds and make them spill forth their wet burden.

Because of the weather several in the group toyed with the idea of staying in their hotel. While most of the pilgrims ventured forth, some of the elderly and a few others stayed behind. Before the day was out they would acknowledge that they had missed a joyous miracle, a Christmas miracle.

Bundled tightly against the plummeting temperatures and the persistent wind, the twelve tourists from Indiana left their hotel. They were nearing the end of their stay in the Holy Land. Today was their last free day for sight-seeing and shopping. They were on their own. They had bid farewell to Adel, their tour guide, the previous evening. With Adel's assistance they had already visited the majority of the accessible religious sights: Bethlehem, Nazareth, the Sea of Galilee, the Jordan, the Dead sea, the Mount of Olives, and the Garden Tomb.

The tensions were great in Israel this year. Israeli hard-liners and Muslim extremists were squaring off on a regular basis. The Gaza area was off limits. So, too, were areas like Hebron where the Patriarchs are believed to be buried. Israeli settlements and Palestinian farming rights constantly made such areas hotbeds of dissent. The Old City, Jerusalem, was a chronic problem. Like a bad case of arthritis it flared up every now and again and made any movement toward peace painful and awkward. Somehow the cold, damp weather forbade such a crippling attack of arthritis.

If the truth were known, many of those who stayed behind in the hotel did so more out of fear than cold.

After buying their tickets stamped "The Ramparts Walk" at the Japha Gate, the small group of twelve began their trek upon the walls of the ancient city. From various vantage points along the wall mosques, church steeples, cemeteries, and even the foundation of the Great Temple could been seen. Three distinct religions—Islam, Judaism, and Christianity—shoulder-to-shoulder, elbow-to-elbow, all visible from the wall.

It was not possible to make the entire circuit around the wall. For safety reasons part of the wall was closed to pedestrian traffic.

There was a great feeling of joy among the twelve. They had been in the Holy Land now for seven days. For many of the group it was like a dream come true, being in Jerusalem and Bethlehem during December. Christmas carols were on their lips as they walked. Some snapped pictures. They were full of joy.

The leader of the group had been here several times He was more quiet. He was trying to figure out the conflicting emotions that were building within him. On the one hand as he looked out over the Old City, he was troubled. "God himself had walked here. Jesus the Messiah had been born near here. Why can't these people see him. Why don't they seek guidance from the Prince of Peace?" The leader's question was so naive. He chided himself. "And besides," he went on in silent conversation, "there is a Christian community down there." He looked down onto the Armenian Quarter. Still he could not shake the growing sense of foreboding.

On the other hand, he was filled with a mysterious sense of joyous anticipation. He joined in with the group as they sang,

> ... the Lord is come.
> Let earth receive her king.
> Let every heart prepare him room.
> And heaven and nature sing,
> and heaven and nature sing,
> and heaven and heaven and nature sing.
>
> Joy to the earth!
> the Savior reigns;
> Let men their songs employ. ...

The leader's attention drifted off in quiet meditation. " 'Joy to the world!' Oh, this world could use some joy."

As he walked he did a mental search through the Scriptures. What had he read in his Advent devotional just that morning? He didn't have the booklet, but he did have his Bible. He dropped his backpack off his shoulder, unzipped it, and pulled out his UltraThin Reference Bible. The wind licked at the pages as he tried to find the words in Isaiah.

> How beautiful upon the mountains
> are the feet of the messenger
> who announces peace,
> who brings good news,
> who announces salvation,
> who says to Zion,
> 'Your God reigns.'
> Listen! Your sentinels
> lift up their voices....

At that precise moment he heard a cry from his group. In his meditation he had wandered on ahead. They had become separated. They were coming near the area where, from the wall, the Western Wall of the Temple could be seen. On the ramparts they were approaching the Dung Gate.

What the leader had not noticed was the armed struggle that was about to take place in the court-yard directly in front of him. It had started as rock throwing from the Muslim-controlled Dome area. Muslims began to enter the Western Wall area. Security guards struggled to contain the flow. In no time the Israeli guards, already on edge, were responding with force. Angry words and rocks from one side; leveled guns on the other. Force seemed destined to be confronted by greater force.

People near the Western Wall were running for cover. They were in a state of panic. There was an electric feeling in the area—the feeling of an execution chair. Someone was going to die. The atmosphere was charged to that extent.

A child, maybe he was ten or so, broke away from his mother and ran straight toward the worsening conflict. His side curls bobbed and his prayer shawl flapped as he ran.

"Oh my God, protect that child," was all the leader could say. He watched the scene in terrified fascination.

The boy ran into the fray. It was an amazing thing to see. The boy somehow maneuvered into the very center of the conflict. The Lord himself seemed to part the way for the child. For a long time the combatants stood toe-to-toe. But now a child stood in between. The child seemed to give each side a reason not to fight, not to shed blood.

An elderly Muslim cleric and a Jewish Rabbi with a gray-streaked beard appeared. They ignored the angry looks of the combatants and walked straight to the boy. Simultaneously, the religious leaders dropped to their knees on the cobblestones of the courtyard. They hugged the child and at the same time their robed arms reached over the child and hugged each other. Tears of repentance began to flow.

Never before had these Muslim and Jewish warriors, who were trained to kill, witnessed such a display. It broke their resolve to fight. Their desire to do damage, take revenge, get the upper-hand, get their rights, and bring peace by force vanished. They looked at the weapons in their hands with growing embarrassment. Soon they could no longer hold their positions of warfare in the face of childlike and child-instituted peace.

Unlike other times, these avowed enemies would never be able to fight again. They had been changed by the courage and love of a child.

In a voice choked with emotion the leader began to read again from Isaiah.

> Listen! Your sentinels
> lift up their voices.
> together they sing for joy;
> for in plain sight they see
> the return of the Lord to Zion.
> Break forth together into singing,

you ruins of Jerusalem;
for the Lord has comforted his people,
he has redeemed Jerusalem.

The leader paused and a woman in the group filled the gap with a reading of her own from Isaiah.

The wolf shall live with the lamb,
the leopard shall lie down with the kid,
the calf and the lion and the fatling together,
and a little child shall lead them.

The cow and the bear shall graze,
their young shall lie down together;
and the lion shall eat straw like the ox.

The nursing child shall play over the hole of the asp,
and the weaned child shall put its hand on the adder's den.

They will not hurt or destroy on all my holy mountain;
for the earth will be full of the knowledge of the Lord
as the waters cover the sea.

On cue, the sun broke through the clouds and bathed the entire Old City in a glorious light. God's pleasure was obvious.

Even the next morning's edition of *The Jerusalem Post* could not refrain from referring to the whole incident as "A Christmas Miracle." And indeed it was.

Cairo, Egypt
December 1994

No one could tell exactly when it had started. It was a gentle murmur—a hum, really. Today we might attribute it to electricity passing through overhead cables or water vibrating some old pipes. Perhaps, if we could come up with no other explanation, we might blame it on an atmospheric disturbance. But the world then was not so advanced as to have harnessed electricity, not so fortunate as to have water singing through metal pipes in poorly insulated walls, not so scientific as to think about atmospheric disturbances.

For those who walked with God the sound was like a mother softly singing to her infant at nap time. It was calming and reassuring. It brought peace and comfort. The sound was thought of as a blessing from God, a gift. For many others who, like Herod, discounted the presence and activity of a holy God, the hum was attributed to evil. It is a noise, an eerie, nerve-jangling, fingernail-on-the-blackboard noise. It made the hair on the back of their necks stand up. It made their skin break out in goose pimples. It was like the painful sound of a dog whistle. It was almost as if the whistle were pitched to a degree of pain in direct correspondence to the extent of their evil.

The hum had started imperceptibly. People went about their business hardly noticing that all nature was tuning up to take part in a glorious fanfare to welcome the Creator. He was coming! The announcement comes through the angel Gabriel. A sparrow sat in the rafters of Mary's home. The bird overheard the words, "Do not be afraid, Mary, for you have found favor with God. And now, you will conceive in your womb and bear a son, and you will call his name Jesus. He will be great, and will be called the Son of the Most High."

The sparrow took to flight. She began to sing forth the marvelous news. "God is now going to send his Son. God is going to do what he promised long ago. The Savior is coming. Our Father is starting his re-creation of all things through his Son." The sparrow's lilting solo was the start of a musical masterpiece.

The news spread quickly. Soon all of creation knew what would soon take place. Rehearsals began. The wind played in the tree branches like a choir of violins. The grasses rustled like castanets. The wolves howled like saxophones. Jackals added their counterpoint. The waterfalls splashed and gurgled. The crow added his minor key. The thunder boomed forth its timpani. All in their separate areas, all warming up, all practicing the music that God had given to their ancestors at the beginning of time. Each had their individual sheets of music. Never had anything in all creation heard what the woods, the winds, the brass, and percussion would sound like when arranged in symphony.

God set the stage in an extravagant way. On a darkened hillside some shepherds were gathering. They had been aware of the humming for months. One would have thought that these illiterate ones would have been superstitious, but not so. They had grown accustomed to nature's participants as they played through their scales and warmed up for the grandest musical production the created order has ever witnessed, let alone participated in. The sheep out on the hillside grew restless. The shepherds' fire crackled and hissed. They were not afraid. On the contrary, they were simply jostling for a better place to see, and even participate in, the symphony. They were looking for the downbeat. They were listening for their cue. Up above, the stars blazed majestically. One star in particular glowed brightly.

Then it happened. An angel with a speaking part. "Do not be afraid; for see—I am bringing you good news of great joy for all people: to you is born this day in the city of David a Savior, who is the Messiah, the Lord." The angel was joined by a vast multitude of the heavenly host praising God and saying,

> Glory to God in the highest heaven,
> and on earth peace among those whom he favors!

And all nature began to sing and dance. Every creature great and small joined in. The musical score was breathtaking. It was joyous and filled to overflowing with God's glory. The mountains and the hills burst forth into song. The trees of the field clapped their hands. The clouds swayed in time with the music. The oceans surged and foamed. A celebration of universal proportions was underway. In no way could it be contained. The long-awaited day of Christ's appearing had come.

At first only a few people heard and understood. They welcomed the chorus. Many rushed to find cotton strips to stuff in their ears. For some, the music drove them mad. In their disturbed state they sought ways to squelch the music, stamp out the joy.

The music plays even still.
The celebration that began on that hillside long ago continues.
The Christ has come.

Do you hear the symphony?

Cairo, Egypt
December 1994

Kingly Discernment

Isaiah 60:1–3, 11; Matthew 2:1–2

The three kings, tribal chieftains really, had known of each other for a long time. To call them friends would have been stretching it, however. On the whole, the three semi-nomadic communities governed by these kings co-existed in peace, perhaps lack of warfare would be a better way to put it. On occasion, scarcity of water and adequate pasture for their herds would ignite a spark of discontent.

The kings did have several things in common. Each wanted the best for his people. Each governed with justice, albeit tribal justice. Each could be described as "a spiritual man"; that is, each had a longing to live in relationship with God. When fear of God was the basic stance of all the tribal peoples round about them, and the belief that God could be manipulated to personal or tribal gain formed the sum total of religious practice, it was quite amazing that these three kings had a deep desire within them to "see God."

It was this intense longing that drew these three chieftains together. They met for the mutual encouragement of their spiritual dreams on the darkest night of every month. You might ask, "Why the darkest?" Because that way, in the midst of the darkness, they would stand a better chance of seeing the glory of God should God decide to make himself known.

When anyone would pass through their territory, the kings would question the travelers regarding their beliefs about God. For the most part they heard the same beliefs over and over. On rare occasions they would hear a new concept, a new idea. Sometimes they were introduced to spiritual writings from peoples far away. Once a caravan came through their region from Jerusalem. They had heard the stories about God shining forth in the darkness, sending a child, a new and mighty king. A king that would govern with justice and mercy. A king that would establish peace for all the world. Now that was the kind of king they were looking for. And to think that these "Children of Israel" would allow anyone access to their coming King!

They often meditated on the words that the traveler had shared with them.

> Arise, shine, for your light has come,
> and the glory of the Lord has risen upon you.
> For darkness shall cover the earth,
> and thick darkness the peoples;
> but the Lord will arise upon you,
> and his glory will appear over you.
> Nations shall come to your light,
> and kings to the brightness of your dawn.

Was it any wonder that they met together on the darkest night of the month? It was at one such meeting that they first saw the star rising. Awe-inspired, each sat transfixed as he gazed at the glowing mass. For well over an hour they sat staring up into the heavens. They had never seen anything like it before. Each one instinctively knew that it was a sign, announcing for all to see, that God was in the process of doing something on a far grander scale than he had ever done before. Just what God was doing, none of these tribal leaders were quite sure.

Dropping his gaze from the heavens and rubbing his aching neck at the same time, the first of the kings asked the obvious, "What does this star mean? What is God trying to tell us?" The answer was as obvious as the questions. Instantly all three men knew what to do. That night each agreed that they would gather not only the resources to travel to Jerusalem but they would also speak to their peoples about what they had seen. "The gifts we carry," they decided, "will come from our people."

Each king returned to his tribe and called the men together. They spoke with great intensity and religious fervor. Their people's spirit caught fire like dry tender. It was a marvelous thing to behold as the people of these three kingdoms gave sacrificially: goats, carpets, jewelry, and bits of highly-valued glass, in order that their representative, their chief, might have a worthy gift to bear to this new born king. In the end, the kings collected all the resources and together bought gold, frankincense, and myrrh.

On the night that the three kings departed, their communities gathered as one to see them off. The elder of the three leaders shared again with the people the words that they had heard long ago from the traveler. He added the words found near the end of the prophesy.

> Your gates shall always be open;
> day and night they shall not be shut,
> so that nations shall bring you their wealth,
> with their kings led in procession.

That these were words about the restoration of Jerusalem, they did not know. Neither did they know how many others they would encounter on their way. They rightly discerned two things about their glorious pilgrimage: they would see God and they would be welcome in his presence.

Cairo, Egypt
December 1994

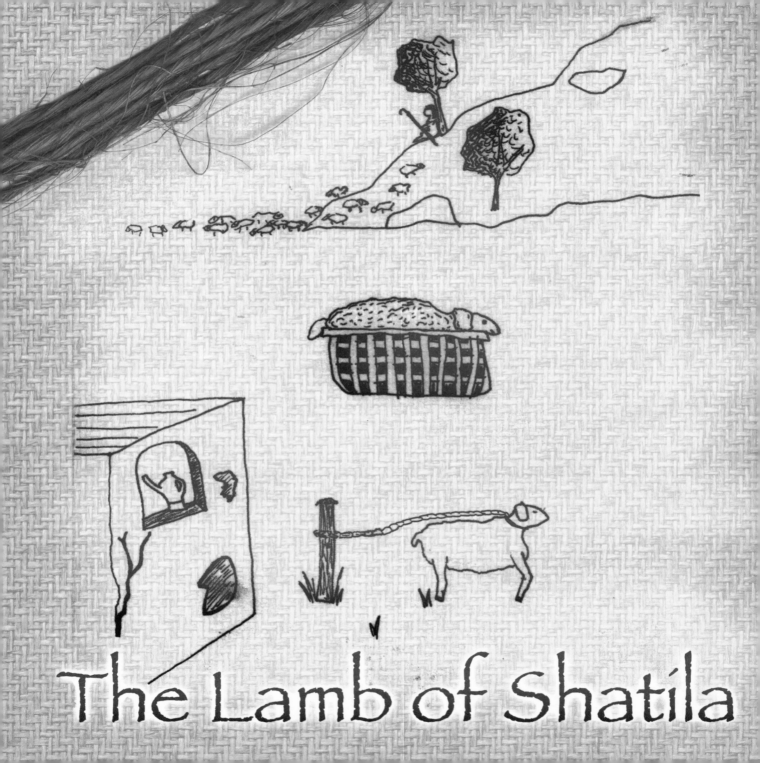

The Lamb of Shatila

t was the summer of 1982. Isa Mubarak was born in a Palestinian refugee camp out in the direction of the Beirut airport. The place was called "Shatila." Isa's parents were "people without papers." They were part of the "Palestinian problem" in Lebanon, stateless refugees in a land at war.

Isa's parents were very poor. They barely made enough to feed themselves. Isa's father worked in a dismal little furniture factory that was located on the road that ran to the airport. He always said that he earned more in splinters than he did in money. In the early weeks and months of her pregnancy, Isa's mother was ill, but when her somewhat frail body adjusted to the pregnancy, she resumed her duties around the house.

House? Did I say "house?" Shed would be more like it. The place where the couple lived was a small little "attachment" to Isa's grandfather's place. The little shed was made of some cast-off bricks and boards. The roof was made from flattened lard tins and cardboard. It was a precarious-looking place. To be honest, the grandfather's place next to it, although just a bit bigger, looked equally unstable. To an outsider it looked as if the shed were the first domino in a series set to cause a chain reaction. That was the way the place looked to an outsider, but then outsiders seldom ventured into the pitiful poverty of the back alleys of Shatila.

Isa was born in this shed. It was not that there were no hospitals available, but who could afford such luxury. The air was heavy and motionless. Distant mortar shells and small arms fire could be heard. Throughout the long afternoon and evening Isa's mother endured an extended labor. As daylight began to break over Shatila, the time of delivery had come. Yet Isa's mother was so drained by the physical strain of labor and the oppressive humidity that she barely had enough energy to push the baby through the birth canal.

When the child was born Isa's "tata" wrapped him in some clean cloths and laid him in a small feedbox near where his mother lay.

The week prior to the birth of Isa, each and every night, the sky over Lebanon was black as pitch and foreboding. It was as if God himself had exerting all his divine energies to assist Isa's mother in preparation for and the delivery of her child. To allow the stars to emit more than a dull grayness seemed as if God's plans might be short-circuited. The creator of light seemed to have issued black out instructions over the war-torn

127

country. The night following the birth of Isa, however, was the opposite to the extreme. The stars were radiant. The sky was awash with light. It was as if all heaven were rejoicing, dancing, celebrating. The intense humidity that ruled both night and day was broken. A breeze, a gentle stirring could be felt. A breath of fresh air touched the face of the mountains in Lebanon.

Out in the Bekaa Valley some Bedouins were tending their sheep. They, more than any others in Lebanon, noticed the change. They were perhaps more attune with nature than anyone else. The previous week their sheep had been restless and irritable. So too were they. Yet on this night things were different. All nature seemed at peace. Their flocks were quiet and peaceful, and God was supplying ample light. They could see to the farthest edges of herd. At midnight shepherd and sheep alike could actually see their shadows. One shepherd among the group had found a rock outcropping and begun to play a lilting tune on his wooden flute. All was at rest on the hillside.

And then the appearance! If the heavens had seemed bright before, now the sky burned with light. The light flashed all about the Bedouins. The Bedouins were terrified. From the center of the light a voice. "Don't be afraid! I have good news for you, which will make everyone happy. This very morning in at the edge of Beirut a child was born. He is Christ the Lord. You will know who he is and you will be able to find him for he will be wrapped in strips of clean cloth and lying in a feedbox." And then suddenly these Bedouins were surrounded by many other angels who sang, "Praise God in heaven! Peace on earth to everyone who pleases God."

As suddenly as they had come, they were gone. Each one of the shepherds had the same thought at the same time. "Let's go to Beirut and see what the mighty God has told us about." They left the sheep in the charge of some of the young boys and began their trek to Beirut. Before leaving the hillside the youngest among the shepherds, the one who would stay and watch the sheep, picked out his favorite lamb, the one he loved and gave it to his father. "Here, father, take this lamb and give it to the baby that the angels told us about." With a smile the father took the perfect little lamb and put it is a blue plastic basket with handles. Then the four Bedouins hurried off on foot to Zahle. From there they were able to catch a service taxi over to Beirut. The ride took forever due to all the military check points on the road. How many times did the four shepherds have to show their identify papers on that ride over the mountain into Beirut? It was a fearsome, hazardous trip.

If ever a city needed to hear a message of peace, it was Beirut. Beirut was the capital of Lebanon, a country at war with itself for years. Israel and Syria had also entered into the conflict. Everyone, every nation, was looking out for their own best interests. Guns and tanks seemed to multiply in direct proportion to the hatred and strife. Intimidation caused hopelessness. Routine death and destruction created a concrete hardness in the people. The Beirut these Bedouins entered was a hell-hole. "Imagine," said one of the three Bedouins crammed in the back of the taxi to the elder of the four who sat in the front seat, "the angel said that a Savior, one who will bring peace, has been born in Beirut!" Without missing a beat the old man in the front responded, "Can you think of a better place and a more appropriate time?" Just at that moment the lamb in the basket grew restless. It bleated several times as if in agreement with what had just been spoken. Then it quieted as the elderly Bedouin stroked its head and spoke tenderly to it.

How these four Bedouins found the small holy family in the refugee camp was amazing. Actually the taxi driver from Zahle had to make several detours to avoid areas of intense fighting. Finally, in fear for his life, he told the Bedouins that they would have to get out and make it on their own. He thought these men must be kind of crazy anyway. They didn't even know where they were going. He was sorry that he had ever agreed to take them. He was thankful for the fare. As if in one quick motion the driver of the service took the money, held the wad of bills up to his forehead then slid them past his rather large nose and kissed it. Then in the blink of an eye, he stuffed the currency in his front shirt pocket, grabbed the gearshift, rammed the car into first gear and was gone in a cloud of dust and choking exhaust. When the dust and pollution settled, the four Bedouins found themselves at the main gate of the Shatila camp.

Not knowing what else to do, the elder of the four men, the one who carried the blue basket with the lamb inside, stopped a group of school-aged boys and asked if they knew of any children that had recently been born in the camp. "Yes," said a twelve-year old boy, "My brother's wife just had a baby the other night."

As the Bedouins followed their new twelve-year old guide back through the dusty, dirty streets of the refugee camp, they wondered silently if this really could be the place. "How can we be going in the right direction?" one mumbled to another. "This child is to be a Savior, a Lord. Who would ever believe that such an important child would be born is a rat-infested place like this?" The elder shushed them. "Remember, my brother, what the angel said, 'You will find the baby wrapped in white cloths and lying in a feed box.' Where in all of Beirut is that more likely than right here in this camp?" The men walked on in silence, a silence that was only broken now and then by the innocent questions of their young guide.

After walking a maze of streets for quite a time, the Bedouins came to a shed that leaned awkwardly to the left. The twelve-year old rushed to find his mother, Isa's grandmother. Over some strong black coffee the Bedouins shared their story of the darkened hillside, the angelic visitors, the hazardous journey, the provision of their young guide. Up to this point the Bedouins had not spoken of the sign, how they would recognize the child when they saw it. "Oh," said the elder Bedouin, "the angel said that we would recognize the child because it would be wrapped in white cloths and would be lying in a feed box." The grandmother kind of jumped as if struck by an uncomfortable shock of electricity. She was on her feet in an instant. "Come and see," were her only words. With that she led the four Bedouins to a curtained off section in the very same room. There behind the curtain was a young woman resting quietly on a small cot. It was obvious from the expression on her face that the new mother had heard everything that the shepherds had said. She smiled a greeting and, without a word, invited these men of the outdoors to look upon her child. Beside the cot was a well-used feed box. In the feed box was an infant wrapped in white strips of cloth sleeping soundly on some clean straw.

The Bedouins did not stay long. They did worship the child in their own quiet way. Before tip-toeing softly from the room, they pronounced words of blessing on the sleeping infant and upon the mother. Then before departing the eldest Bedouin picked up the blue plastic basket and gave it to the grandmother. "This lamb is from my son to your grandson. He wanted to give this lamb for he loves it with all his heart." The gift of the lamb was received with great tenderness. Tears were in the eyes of the grandmother.

The trip back over to the Bekaa seemed short. The Bedouins were filled with a great and unexplainable joy. They shared about the baby and the angels visit with everyone they met. What a reunion back on the hillside with the youngest shepherd and the family left behind! They told every detail with great joy. "The savior of the world has come!" they announced. "We know it because what we heard about we have now seen." The youngest shepherd was particularly happy to know that his gift had been so warmly received.

Summer seemed long that year. The war continued. Tensions were great. The Israelis had invaded Lebanon earlier that year. By August the French peacekeepers were withdrawn. The PLO was also forced to leave. Things in the refugee camp were uneasy at best.

. . . . .

During the days of early September three very dignified men appeared at the gate to Shatila. Some people thought they were UN aid workers; others took them for reporters. These men were neither. These men were persons who had been awaiting for the birth of this holy child. Strangely enough they had seen a star in the heavens. They understood the star's significance. All three men—one a Coptic Christian from Cairo, one a believer from the United States, and the third a lay evangelist from Singapore—met in Cyprus and took a boat to Juniya.

These men, like the Bedouins before them, came to worship the child. They brought valuable gifts and, more importantly, information. After worshiping the child, they gathered in the main part of the house and talked with the family. The Coptic Christian from Egypt translated. "You must leave this place," the lay evangelist said. "Yes," said the American believer, "we had a dream. You cannot stay here. The evil one himself is at work at this very moment to kill your child."

"How can we leave?" asked the carpenter father. "We have no money and we have no papers. Who would accept us? Where could we go?" There was a desperation in his voice.

"Come to Egypt," said the Copt. "I have connections. I believe we can get you visas."

"As far as money, we will provide for your passage," said the lay evangelist.

"This is foolishness," said the grandmother. "These children of mine will not go anywhere." It was obvious that when she spoke she expected to be obeyed. It was then that the grandfather spoke, "My dear," he said gently to his wife, "these men are offering to help baby Isa and his parents. We would be foolish not to allow them to go." With that, the matter was settled. It took a few days to arrange the paperwork and passage to Egypt. The holy family was able to escape Lebanon the very day Bashir Gemayel was assassinated.

Two days later, Friday, September 17, Israeli soldiers closed off the Shatila camp. No one was allowed to enter or exit. All that night the sky was lighted with phosphorous shells. Militia men were inside the camp. For three days the Shatila camp became the sight of a massacre. Death was everywhere. Shatila had become a gruesome place.

After three days the Israeli soldiers who encircled Shatila and the fighters inside the camp pulled out and away from the area. When the doors were opened and reporters were permitted inside, the world became aware of what had happened. The journalist who reported the scene wrote this on the front page of *The Herald Tribune*.

"On a back street of the Shatila camp tied to a rusty pole next to a ramshackle shed was a small white lamb. The lamb had been slain, its white wool stained by its crimson blood. Innocence and purity was sacrificed. Oh, that this lamb could atone for the sins committed in Shatila. Oh, that the blood of this lamb could take away the sins of all the world."

What this journalist didn't realize was that the boy born just days before the massacre was indeed the very lamb of God sent to be God's decisive sacrifice for all sin, everywhere, including that which was committed in Shatila.

Beirut, Lebanon
December 1996

A Story Woven From Philippian Threads

The Earthenware Jar

od's throne room was not a room at all. To call it a room was to give in to the desire to attempt to describe the unfathomable. It was a vast open space of universal, unbounded proportions. After all, what kind of throne room could contain a God of such infinite immensity, power, and majesty?

In the center of the eternal openness was a throne unlike any ever imagined by monarch or craftsman. Its massiveness was evident. It had a bright and holy quality about it that shimmered and sparkled to such an extent that gazing upon it was painful to the eye. The message it reflected was about God's character. The sovereign King who occupied this throne was awesome in power and pristine in holiness.

Next to the massive throne was a brass, three-legged table that looked like it belonged in some Middle Eastern coffee shop. It was as plain and ordinary as God's throne was massive and ornate. On this circular table was a brownish, well-formed, and totally unremarkable earthenware jug. The jug seemed to be some sort of out-of-place souvenir, as if God had traveled to any one of a thousand market places and purchased the jug on a whim. Talk about out of place! That jug didn't seem to belong in that throne room any more than dirt and clutter did.

No one dared to ask God why the earthenware jug was set beside his throne. In the eyes of the heavenly hosts, the jug seemed to disgrace the throne and the room. All of the angel army wondered and some even speculated that perhaps the jug was a symbol of the coming judgment. Maybe at the end of time God would reach for the pot and shatter it into a million never-to-be recreated pieces. Or maybe it was some sort of divine prop which God would ceremoniously use to once-and-for-all wash his hands of his hell-bent humanity.

· · · · ·

Gathering his splendor around him as the morning horizon gathers the dawn, God spoke. His prophets, ever attuned to his voice, heard and repeated his message.

For a child has been born to us,
A son given to us;
Authority rests upon his shoulders;
And he is named
Wonderful Counselor, Mighty God,
Everlasting Father, Prince of Peace.
His authority shall grow continually,
And there shall be endless peace
For the throne of David and his kingdom.
He will establish and uphold it
With justice and righteousness
From this time onward and forevermore.

But you, O Bethlehem of Ephrathah,
Who are one of the little clans of Judah,
From you shall come forth for me
One who is to rule in Israel,
Whose origin is from of old,
From the ancient of days.

All of the heavenly army was placed on alert. God was about to act. He intended to do something unimaginable.

God summoned his Son. God's throne room was filled to capacity with heaven's army standing at attention, eager for action, ready to fulfill any command their Lord and Master might decree. The excitement was electric. As the Son strode in wrapped in confidence and holiness, silence washed across the throne room like a mighty incoming tide.

God spoke not a word. Instead he reached for the earthenware jug and slowly and methodically began to pour the liquid contents on to the marble floor. The Son, as if in rehearsed and choreographed reply, smiled, turned on his heels, departed, descended, not to return again until he had completed that task for which he was being sent.

Gabriel was sent forth to speak to a priest, a virgin, and the man she was intending to marry. An amazing star was hung in the heavens. The entire heavenly host was dispatched to split the night sky with light and sound. And what a sound! Heavenly anthems sung to down-and-out shepherds.

The earthenware jug that had confused and confounded the heavenly hosts for uncountable ages became a clear and compelling reason to sing. God's Son would take the form of earthly humanity so that humanity could understand God's message. Everything fit together as tightly as a puzzle crafted before creation. Well, almost everything. "Why," whispered some angels among themselves, "had God poured the liquid from the jug?" The answer became obvious to all in the short span of human history. The message of that jug being poured out became clear as glass. God's Son became man to empty himself to redeem God's fallen children.

One human writer would later record about the Son that "Though he was in the form of God, he did not regard equality with God something to be exploited, but emptied himself, taking the form of a slave, being born in human likeness. And being found in human form, he humbled himself and became obedient to the point of death—even death on a cross."

Rome, Italy
October 1999